Never Again

by

Steve Anthony

Copyright © 2019 Steve Anthony

ISBN: 978-0-244-19418-5

All rights reserved, including the right to reproduce this book, or portions thereof in any form. No part of this text may be reproduced, transmitted, downloaded, decompiled, reverse engineered, or stored, in any form or introduced into any information storage and retrieval system, in any form or by any means, whether electronic or mechanical without the express written permission of the author.

Dedication

This book is for Samantha and Carly, with much love.

Front cover illustration by

Mick Daines.

In The Beginning....

I was George Best. At least, I used to *think* I was George Best. I was also at various times Alan Ball, John Connolly or Joe Royle.

I used to think I was me. But I was wrong.
I was fourteen years old when everything in my world changed.

I was out on the grass in front of my house, playing football, with my best friend Mark and a couple of mates. I was dribbling the ball, kicking it against our hedge and getting ready to flick it over Mark's head. Something made me look up.

At the front bedroom window, with the curtain open, was my Dad looking down at me.

He lifted his finger, beckoning me to come in.

My heart sank. 'Fuck,' I thought, 'He must have heard me swearing.'

I didn't know what I'd done yet, but I knew I had to be in trouble.

I went in and Dad told me to sit down.

"W-w-what have I d-d-done wrong?" Were the first words out of my mouth. In fact, that was always the first thing I asked when I thought I was in trouble. And the stammer made a regular appearance too. I stammered a lot back then, especially when I was nervous. But Dad didn't answer, not the way I expected. This clearly wasn't the usual telling off.

"I've a story to tell you," Dad said. This wasn't normal. I hadn't a clue where he was going with this.

"A few years ago, there was a man and a woman," Dad continued, "And they had a boy and girl…"

"W-w-who's the b-b-boy?" I asked instinctively. I hadn't thought that the boy might be me; it was just the first thing that came out.

"Let me tell it how I'm telling it," Dad raised his hand for silence and carried on, without any more interruptions from me.

He continued with his story. He told me how this man and this woman eventually decided they didn't get on and, when they split up, it was decided that the woman would take the girl and the man would take the boy. Both the man and woman found other partners and married again and raised new families of their own. And the boy? The boy was me.

It was like a hammer blow. Everything I thought I knew fell apart.

I did cry, not because I was upset, or at least I don't think so but more because it seemed like the thing to do. Shock was the main thing I was feeling.

My Dad carried on telling me about the family I didn't know I had, filling in the gaps. I had a sister, two years older than me, in Scunthorpe, and my own four sisters, here, were my half-sisters. In addition to that, I had four stepsisters in Scunthorpe, living with my birth Mum.

My own sisters hadn't been told yet; they were all a bit young. But my real sister, in Scunthorpe knew and had said she wanted to meet me.

While I was still reeling from it all, Dad then got to the crux of why he was telling me this. My Mum, or who I'd thought was my real Mum, with me getting older, would probably hear; 'You don't look old enough to have had Stephen'.

And that was that. World changed.

"Now go to bed," Dad drew it to a close with an oft used command, even though it was only four in the afternoon. "Your Mum's at the shops. She'll come up to see you when she's done. You need to tell her it doesn't make any difference and she's still your Mum."

As I lay on my bed, bright afternoon light streaming in through the window, a lot of things seemed to become clear. It wasn't just this new information changing my perspective. I never got on with my mother, we had constant run ins, arguments that saw me going to my room to punch the walls or smash something of my own, just to release my anger and frustration. And my sisters? They never got told off, not that I remember, only ever me.

I sometimes felt like I lived in a house full of people but all on my own. And now I knew why. She wasn't my mother. It seemed to make sense we didn't get on – at least to my young mind, it was easier to hang things on that assumption.

Eventually she knocked on my door and came in, sitting on the edge of my bed.

"Has your Dad told you?" she asked.

"Yeah."

And then she reached out for me, putting her arms around me and giving me a hug.

I can't remember her ever hugging me before.

Before I could get over the shock of this she spoke again, arms still around me.

"Just because I'm not your real mother," she said, "It doesn't mean I can stop telling you off."

Incredible! Of all the things to say in that moment. With hindsight, I like to think it was maybe a throwaway comment, designed to lighten the mood. The trouble with hindsight though – it doesn't come till later. Much later in my case. And that comment stayed with me all my life.

Even at that age I could tell she'd just handed me a shit sandwich. I couldn't win. Fair enough she wasn't my real Mum, but she did still get to tell me off.

In years to come that stammering, angry teenager, desperate to be loved and feeling alone would be hard to reconcile with the young able seaman fearlessly piloting a dinghy on the open seas, the radar operator trusted by the skipper for difficult channel crossings, the ladies' man with conquests across the Western hemisphere or the award winning stage and screen actor.

But the journey through all those things seemed to start here, in this moment, being handed this shit sandwich. It might sound trite but it's true - the search for love and acceptance that drove me, for bad and for good, for the rest of my young adult life, began with this unwelcome news that caused everything to change.

Growing Up

Up until my teens I'd never been the popular one in school. Not by a long way. I wore big Joe 90 glasses – trendy today - and carried a briefcase (not by personal choice) neither of which made me an obvious candidate for being cool. On top of that was my stutter. It was bad and worse when I was nervous or under pressure and whilst at primary school, they had tried several things to cure it.

One of the standout ways they tried this was getting me to perform in front of the whole school. Back then, for some reason, they were sure getting me to read out a passage in assembly, in front of all the other students and teachers, would help me control my speaking. I was around ten at the time.

I still remember how well I thought I'd done at self-consciously trying to make my way through the reading, taking it slowly, trying to make it through without stuttering. In my head it had gone brilliantly but when I asked my friends how I'd done it turned out that I'd stuttered the whole way through, I was just so used to it I hadn't even noticed.

At home things weren't much better. In fact, I still think the atmosphere of tension at home is what caused the stammer in the first place. As I said, I argued a lot with my Mum and was also the only one asked to do anything around the house, like washing and drying the pots before I was allowed out or babysitting my younger sisters, or to get a telling off. And I seemed to get told off all the time.

One side effect of me getting told off all the time was a defensive reaction of constant lying. My first reaction to any accusation became to lie, immediately, automatically, no matter what. And I had a good memory for the lies I told. Mostly.

There was one time I was babysitting, left home alone while Mum and Dad went down the pub. Before they left Dad loomed over me, 6'4", ex-rugby player and, to this day, the only man I've ever been physically afraid of, and gave me an instruction not to eat any fried egg sandwiches.

I had a penchant for fried egg sandwiches at the time, but Dad was looming over me and telling me the eggs were needed for whatever they were needed for, so I told him that, yeah, yeah, of course I wouldn't.

The minute, the very minute, he was gone; I went to the kitchen, broke two eggs, fried them up and made myself a fried egg sandwich, leaving the shells in a blue tin Jubilee Stout ashtray which Dad had brought back from the pub. I don't know why I cooked 'em, I never even thought about it.

About half ten, Mum and Dad got back. I was lying on the floor watching telly, with my head on a cushion as my Dad came in and towered over me.

"I thought I told you not to have any fried egg sandwiches," he said.

"I've not!" I said, not even thinking about it, the lie going out ahead of me, tripping off my tongue – and tripping me up.

He didn't speak.

There was a sharp burst of pain as he kicked me in the thigh. Then he leaned down and picked me up off the floor, dragging me into the kitchen.

"What the fuck's that then?" he said, jabbing his finger at the ashtray full of eggshells.

My mouth flapped open, the stammer and fear stopping me from getting any words out.

He gave me a clout and then up I went to bed. It seems funnier now, and I'm still not sure why I lied to him when I should have known I'd be caught. But it was part of a pattern. Dad was good at picking the best moment to catch me out.

I lived with my Gran and Granddad for a while when I was younger, and it wasn't until later that I moved back in with Mum and Dad. I stayed close to them and I used to go to my Granny Smart's house every Saturday and do her shopping for her.

I'd go to the chemists/book shop, with its larger print easy reader books, and loan her out one of those and buy her a bottle of linctus, cough medicine, although she never had a cough, she just used to glug it. It was addictive stuff back then.

Alongside the money for her shopping she also used to give me sixpence or a shilling for my troubles. On this one occasion, when I was about twelve, and a couple of weeks before I was due to go on holiday, she gave me five shillings. At that age, back in the day, that was a fortune. But that didn't stop me from spending it all in one go. I bought a humongous amount of sweets, including four or five crème eggs and nearly made myself ill eating them all.

That evening I was in the front room with Mum and Dad, sat on the settee watching telly. Dad was sat in a separate chair, dead silent as we all watched whatever was on. This was textbook. He had a knack for waiting for an opportune moment to strike, like now, in the middle of a drama when I was in the zone, totally absorbed in the program.

Right out of the blue Dad suddenly spoke.

"Where's your holiday money?"

I froze.

"Where's your holiday money?"

I tried to speak but, as usual, couldn't get my words out.

"Joan," Dad turned to my Mum, "Turn the television off."

I started panicking then.

"Where's your holiday money?"

"W-w-what h-h-holiday m-m-money?"

"The five shillings your Gran gave you this morning," he kept on, "For your holiday."

There was no escape.

"I spent it."

"What on?"

"Sweets," I said sheepishly, although the instinct to protect myself jumped in, "I gave some away!"

It was a valiant attempt to offset some of the blame by showing my kindness; by saying I didn't eat them all. I did eat them all.

It was obvious I was in for a leathering. He grabbed me and in desperation I reached for my Mum, the bystander as always, and got hold of the sleeve of her cardigan as he lifted me up. I held on so tight that I pulled the cardigan off her as Dad dragged me off the settee.

As he pushed me up the stairs in front of him, it seemed like he whacked me on every stair and by the time he got me to my room it was hurting badly enough that I tried to stand up to him.
"That's enough!" I pleaded, hoping he'd agree.
"I'll fucking tell you when you it's enough." He said.
It's testament to the awesomeness of Crème Eggs that I can still eat them now.

Teeny Bopper

Later, after the big change in my life, I had a house party when my Mum and Dad went on holiday and left me alone in the house. We had a sideboard drinks cabinet in the front room, one of those you pull out and the light comes on, with bottles of Matteus Rose, (among others) in the wicker basket weave, from back when you could only ever get it on holiday.

As you might expect with a house party, we emptied the lot. Every bottle. Obviously, I panicked when I realised what we'd done. I mean, how was I going to cover it up? So, I did what seemed obvious at that moment. I just filled the bottles up with water. Some of them hadn't been touched in years, so surely nobody would notice.

At that party I'd also discovered, hidden at the back out of sight in the glory hole, the cupboard in the kitchen, a dark bottle with chalk around the top.

I'd given the drink, which later turned out to be really, expensive port, a quick taster - made a face at how disgusting it was, and then poured it down the sink, thinking it must have gone off.

After Mum and Dad got back I didn't think anything else of what I'd done. They didn't say anything about the drink's cabinet (why would they?) and everything seemed ok.

One evening a week later, a full week, we were sat watching telly and Dad turned to me and said;

"Go get me a drink of brandy, Stephen."

"Yeah, alright," I didn't even think about it. Then, as I was walking to the cabinet, I remembered. Fuck. There's nothing in there!

Even now I can feel him behind me, waiting. It's funny to remember now but then, I was papping myself.

I poured him his drink. What else could I do?

"What's this?" he asked.

"Water…" I said, shame faced.

But it didn't end there.

"A little while ago," Dad continued, "My boss, the director of my company gave me a bottle of port. About fifty pounds a bottle Stephen..."

It had to be that bottle from the glory hole. He knew.

"I-i-it was all mouldy," I tried to justify myself, "Around the top of the bottle."

"That wasn't mould, son. That was chalk, to protect the cork," Dad still hadn't got the answer he was looking for, "Where is it?"

"I didn't like it..." I said looking at my feet, "So I poured it down the sink."

You can imagine what came next. World War Three.

But what got me was the timing of it, waiting a week to catch me out, when he must have known all along. I've often thought that, if I wanted to mentally torture someone that would be the way to do it just leaving them hanging, waiting to see if they'd get caught.

I still don't know why I refilled those bottles with water. I must have known I'd get caught.

All the way through school I'd been in the A stream and, like I said, wearing Joe 90 glasses and carrying the briefcase Mum and Dad made me take to school.

One day, aged around fourteen and a half, everything changed. I didn't know why. It was like somebody had flicked a switch. One morning, as I got ready for school, I just put my normal clothes on, instead of my school uniform; I didn't wear my glasses and I left my briefcase at home.

It was a massive change. In pretty short order, I went from being someone that wasn't noticed to being invited to spend time in the girl's cloak room. It really affected my mother; she couldn't understand what had happened and it became increasingly clear she resented the change. There seemed to be constant friction between us.

When I argued with my Mum, I needed an outlet for the anger. I'd punch the wall, and sometimes, as I got older, right in front of her face. Mostly I'd go up to my room and break something of my own, just to get out my frustration. I wouldn't have dared laid a finger on her, no matter how angry I got, I knew Dad would've killed me. If somebody needed to intercede to end the argument it would be my Dad. And he made it perfectly clear where he stood between the three of us. If anything was going to give, if anyone had to change, it had to be me. Dad made it perfectly clear, that, if it came to it, he'd pick her before he'd pick me. For her part, Mum was totally devoted to Dad; subservient to him really, it seemed to me. But what did I know? I was only a kid and saw only black or white and not the 'big picture'. It wasn't until he passed away that she managed (needed) to find her own independence.

As scared as I was of my Dad at times, I did once discover that he wasn't without his weaknesses.

The house we lived in had a real fire in the front room. To get the coal for it you had to go out to the outhouse, which was through the dining room, past the hallway and kitchen and then it was just outside the back door.

One night I was upstairs, and I heard him in the front room say he was going to get the coal in. I crept downstairs and hid behind the door jamb of the kitchen into the hallway.

The house was in the pitch dark and I just saw Dad's shadow come through the kitchen door. I waited until I saw the tip of the coal shovel just appearing in front of me and then jumped out with a 'RAAAR'.

The coal flew straight up in the air. I caught the look on his face. It was the only time I've ever seen him startled. The coal went everywhere, all over the kitchen floor.

Of course, I had to run then. I was out the house and then up the drainpipe like the proverbial rat, to the flat roofed outbuilding that backed onto my bedroom. Once I was up there I was stuck.

"I can't get up there," Dad called up, "But I can wait till you come down!"

I must have stayed there for about 2 hours. But his anger eventually wore off or else he saw the funny side, as I don't remember getting punished for that.

For me though, it had been a real surprise to see that look of shock on my Dad's face.

With the change that came over me, ditching the Joe 90 glasses and briefcase, I found myself starting to stick up for myself too.

My Mum's brothers, my uncles Geoff and Mark (who were pretty much the age of cousins, three or four years older than me) had always teased me, relentlessly all my childhood. But, by the age of fourteen and a half, I wanted it to change.

Geoff's thing was chasing me with spiders. Daddy Long Legs that he found on the wall outside our house. On this one occasion he chased me round the house and up the stairs. This time I'd had enough. Fed up and angry, I turned around and pushed him, sending him falling backwards down the stairs.

Also, in the house was one of my Mum's older brothers, Jim, an ex-marine, who came running at the sound of the fall.

"What's going on?" he was furious, I could tell he was holding himself back, "You could have killed him!"

"I've had enough!" I shouted, "I've had enough!"

The emotion, the frustration was genuine. As angry as Uncle Jim was, he could see I meant it. Geoff must have too because he didn't chase me any more after that.

Not long after I was at a family party at my house and my other uncle, Mark was up to his usual tricks, this time kneeing me on the back. It had happened enough in the past but, like I say, I'd had enough by then.

And, unfortunately for Mark, by then I'd been having martial arts lessons.

As he kneed me, I turned around, grabbing him, and threw him over my hip. He flew across the room and crashed down on to the floor. He was shocked and clearly properly hurt.

"What the hell are you doing?" Mum and the other adults had seen the whole thing and were as shocked as Mark, "What was that for?"

"I'm fed up!" I started shouting then and kept shouting, too fed up to be scared of making a scene, "Everyone's always going at me! It's always me! Why's it always me?!"

And, as much as I had caused a scene, it worked. The teasing stopped. Neither of them came at me again.

12

Handsome Young Devil

As I said, I'd started learning karate and kung fu, back in around 1973. I think I'd perceived I wasn't part of the popular crowd and I did it ostensibly because I was mad keen on Bruce Lee, not that I'd really been bullied at all.

I went all in, like with pretty much everything I do, taking it to extremes. So, I went to Shukokai karate 2 or 3 times a week and, even when I wasn't there, I'd practice all the time in my bedroom at home. I spent most of my time alone in my room at home anyway, so I had nothing else to do but spend two or three hours a night practising kata and techniques in front of the mirror. And so, as you might expect, I got really good, and really fast.

On the way back from practise one night I was seen at the village square bus stop by a lad called Colm – one of the popular set. He asked where I'd been and I never really mixed with any of the popular crowd in those days, so they wouldn't know, and it seemed an innocent enough question, so I told him I'd been to karate.

"Oh aye, with so-and-so?" he mentioned the tutor, who everyone in the village knew, essentially because the guy was reckoned to be a tad over the top with his training methods.

I nodded nonchalantly but Colm kept on, clearly intrigued that I would do karate.

"So, if I threw a punch you could block it?" he said.

"Yeah," I shrugged again.

"Really? So, if I went for you then, like now, you could stop me?"

"Yeah, yeah."

This would come to be a defining moment in my school life, not that I knew it then. But I knew I could block him, and he had asked, so, to demonstrate, I took up a defensive stance and he squared up opposite me.

"Whenever you're ready." I said, "Punch."

He threw a punch and, of course, I saw it coming a mile away. Quick as anything, and before he knew anything about it, my hand came up and blocked it.

"Fucking hell" Colm's jaw was on the floor, "Fucking hell! That's fucking *amazing*! Can you do that again?!"

"I can do it as many times as you like." I shrugged.

Word soon got around, Colm telling everyone what I could do, telling everyone that Utting was like lightning, like fucking Bruce Lee.

I was getting known, and it wasn't a bad thing.

Being known also helped with the girls, which I was getting increasingly interested in.

At around the same age was when I lost my virginity too. I used to go to a club on Saturday afternoons run by Radio Humberside. Interestingly in 1974 they had a competition - junior DJ of 1974. You had to pick a record to play and write something around it as an introduction and read it out. That then went out on the air and the audience in the club had to vote for who they liked the best. It was a bit like Opportunity Knocks and the clapometer – you know, the louder the claps…

Now, I didn't see it in those days, but I was very personable and likeable, regardless of all my issues. It might have been obvious to others that I'd do well but it wasn't to me, I might well have been personable, but I didn't see it. I was pretty much on the borderline of insecurity and finding my feet. I imagine most teens feel the same at some point.

The song I chose was Dave Edmund's Rockpile – I Hear You Knocking. I don't really remember what I said to introduce it, but the audience all voted for me. I was amazed, I couldn't believe it, out of all the people in the competition, they picked me.

That was one of only a few things I've ever won in my life. The first was a set of glasses at a bingo competition whilst on a family holiday. It was a set of tumblers with rainbow patterns and I thought 'Mum would love these'. And then, proudly carrying them on the way back to the caravan, I went and dropped them breaking the lot. I don't think mum and dad really believed me.

'I won you some glasses! But I dropped them...'

'Right... Well done son...'

The other thing was when I was in the navy, on board the ship. Over the ship's in-house radio/TV, a question was asked 'Mungo Jerry had only one other number one apart from In the Summertime, what was it?' And I knew it, it was Baby Jump, just one of those obscure bits of pop trivia you remember, so I was looking around to see if anybody else knew or was going to do anything about it. Nobody but me seemed to know so I went off and claimed my prize, some cans of ale, as I recall.

For the junior DJ 1974 competition, the prize was a choice between two albums; either Cheap Trick or Kraftwerk. I picked the Kraftwerk one, not really knowing what it was. But wow. It was incredible. It was Autobahn and I must have played that record every day for a year.

At that club, there was this girl who was older than me. She was 17 and a *woman*. She came up to me and asked if I wanted to come babysitting with her that night. Never imagining what would happen, I said yeah.

Her Mum went out and almost immediately she handed me a key.

"Go and lock the door," she said.

I had an idea of what was up then.

When we got down to it, I remember feeling between her legs and thinking 'bloody hell, I'm not sure I can touch the sides!' she was quite Amazonian, you see, really stacked. But that didn't stop me.

It was amazing.

But it was also a bit bittersweet. She got off really quickly, and then it was then a case of 'Have you done yet' from her, all the while I'm thinking 'this is amazing! I could do this all night!' Which, of course, you can at that age, can't you?

I remember going home in the morning thinking, 'Fucking hell! Done it!' But then it was a teeny bit of a downer thinking of how quickly it was over. After all that build up it felt like a bit of a gip.

Not long after that I didn't want to see her anymore. I took her to the school disco and everyone there older than me was trying to get off with her – which was slightly weird. It wasn't a malicious thing. But we'd done it and she hadn't really seemed that into it and I hadn't got a lot from her.

About a week or so after I had packed her in, I got a phone call telling me she was pregnant. I remember telling my mum – just as a heads up, in case it was true, and mum nearly passed out. Obviously, it turned out she wasn't, and it was just a ploy to fuck me up. It wasn't the only time I've had a woman seem not that into me and then not wanting to let me go.

Around this time was also when I first met my real mum, which was an amazing but also unsettling experience.

Meeting my real mum was a weird experience. We met and immediately hugged; it was very loving, but very strange too. Here was a stranger, who I didn't know at all, giving me these warm hugs and telling me she loved me, etc. It didn't seem an issue that she hadn't bothered with me until then – but again, what did I know?

My half-sisters were all very pretty and excited to have a brother for the first time. We went down the pub and I was really confused to be getting jealous stares and comments from people in the bar for all the attention I was getting from the girls. They were naturally touchy-feely, not in a weird way, but it clearly made some of the locals jealous. I'd protest that I was their brother, but the blokes were all sneery, saying, 'Yeah but you're not really though, are you? You're their half-brother.'

Even with that negativity, I had a great time in Scunthorpe. Everybody loved me there, because I was the brother they never knew they had.

On top of that, I was the centre of attention, which was new to me, something I'd never had, never been before. It was amazing. But it fucked me up. There were lots of confusing thoughts and no one to speak to about them.

After getting that love and affection and attention, I didn't want it to stop. I wanted that feeling all the time. It was like an addiction.

This would profoundly affect my relationships from then on. Throughout my life I've always told girls how much I like them, how important they are to me, not just to get them into bed but because I really meant it. And I really did. In that moment. It's only the next morning that I move on and look for that hit of love and attention from someone else. Sincerity. Winner, winner.

But at that time, I just wanted the intensity of that feeling of attention and went all in for it. I had two proper relationships at school, and they were both about six months long, which at that age, in school, was a long time. With both they were everything in and that's how I've always been.

But for my first girlfriend I dated a popular girl. That was probably a mistake in hindsight. In the end she binned me for being too nice.

I didn't really know what to do, I wasn't certain, wasn't sure of me or how to be. She probably just wanted shagging, really, but I wasn't in the right state of mind for that then.

She was good about it, though.

'Look Steve, you're really nice, but...'

But that was that. I was binned.

She was right, though. It got quite intense after that, as soon as I was single again. I had a lot of girls calling for me.

Mum was really displeased at all the attention and affection I was getting. When she answered the phone to any of the girls I had calling for me, and I had a lot of girls phoning me, she'd call for me by shouting – "Stephen, it's another one of your Harem for you!" followed by the girl on the phone asking what Mum had just called her.

"What did she call me?!"

"Don't worry about it..."

Of course, Mum describing all the girls calling for me as my harem was just a joke but there was genuinely real bitterness in it. Even then I couldn't help thinking, why can't you just be happy for me? These people want me!

My sister Alison also brought some friends home who I ended up going out with, so maybe there was a bit of distrust sown there, too.

But there was no doubt, by this point, that I was popular. On one occasion the head of year, Mr Whitlock (or Peg Leg as we called him then - because of his club foot - which we really shouldn't have, as he was a lovely, lovely man) came and found me and my mate Troy in the girl's cloakrooms. We weren't allowed to be in there, but we went in because that's where all the girls where, Duh! And Mr. Whitlock clearly knew that would be the best place to find us.

He came up to the end of the row and popped his head round.
"Stephen, Troy, I need to talk to you, I need your help!" the girls were all goggle-eyed, wondering what was going on. "Come on, come out, you're not meant to be in here anyway."

Troy and I had had a date swap the night before, just for a giggle, him going out with my date and me going out with his. Now, legend had it, the girls were wanting to swap again, they both liked us but they were arguing over who was going to see who, and Mr Whitlock had come to ask us to talk to them before the next class as it was disrupting the lessons.

Being 14, with supreme confidence we were all, 'we'll do what we can sir'. And of course, we told everyone all around the school in about a minute.

'Yeah, yeah, we've got to sort out some girls who are causing some grief, Mr Whitlock's asked us to sort it out for him.'

That really enhanced our reputation at school!

I met Troy around the same time as my step-change. I was waiting outside class reception, when this guy came up to me and said "eyup Steve, I'm Troy". I had never seen or noticed him before, and I asked him how he knew my name. "It's written on your arm" he replied. It was the thing back then to write or carve your name on your arm (don't ask me why).

We hit it off straight away and he was my best mate for a couple of years till we left school. He was also a right handsome devil and we made a great team.

But as much as i played the field, I was still everything in when it came to some relationships, as was proved by Marianne. She was my second proper girlfriend, lasting about 6 months and she was my first real love.

She was gorgeous, her breath tasted of Juicy Fruit and she had a bubble cut haircut and elfin face. I wrote a song about her years later, called Ice Cream, summing up what she meant to me. It was intense.

When she packed me in I was devastated. It was a weight on my mind for over twenty years after, thinking about what might have been, where she was, what she was doing - genuinely not a week would go by where I didn't think of her.

It was a weight on my mind, a cloud hanging over me, the constant 'what if, what if, and what if'. I loved her bitterly.

About twenty-five years later I was at my Mum's for a weekend and I took a phone call. It was my sister;

"I'm at Hessle High School Reunion," Mandy said, "You'll never guess who I'm stood with."

And of course, I knew.

"Is it Marianne?"

"Yeah. You coming up?"

I was out of the house in about thirty seconds.

I drove up and met our Mandy and immediately started looking round the classroom for any sight of Marianne.

"Where is she?" I asked.

"She's there," Mandy pointed at someone. Someone who I didn't even recognise.

And the relief! She looked nothing like Marianne, the girl who had haunted my thoughts for all those years. The pressure and the wanting and the longing that had been on me just dissipated. I looked in her eyes and I couldn't see her. That Marianne wasn't there.

It was bittersweet but it was genuinely such a relief. The weight I'd been carrying for twenty-five years was gone.

As a teenager, I also started working, part time, and this soon overlapped with my burgeoning love life. My ex-marine Uncle was a sales director for Eden Vale, so he got me my first part time job as a van lad, delivering yoghurts. We used to go all the way up the east coast ending up in Scarborough, delivering to the holiday camps on the way. We would stay in digs in Scarborough and then come back.

There was me with my pigeon chest, a duster coat and no top on, with big sideburns, more hair then than I've ever had in my life, thinking I was Tarzan but looking more like a rooster.

The driver, Russell, was the exact spitting image of Noddy Holder and he was a serious lady's man, and good at it. He used to drive a yellow Vauxhall Firenza, Vauxhall's sports car back in the day and every shop we went in the girls were always all over him.

I'd got into the mode of pulling women, or what I then called 'trapping', by then, and Russell was the same. So, when we got to Scarborough, we had competitions.

We'd start at one end of the town and work our way along, seeing who, in the next three hours could get the most girls to kiss them and take their picture with us (and we had to get a photo taken in a booth to qualify). And they were big numbers.

The person I was then, I couldn't do it now. But then I had nothing but confidence to do it. After my relative success at school and after losing my virginity, my confidence deffo took a step up. I used to walk down the amusements and I'd have my eye on a girl. As I got close I'd smile at her. When I walked past her I'd go about ten paces and then look behind me quickly. Nine times out of ten she'd be looking back, so I knew she was interested. I would then nod at the amusements and infer we would meet inside. It was a tried and trusted method and I did it every single time.

I'd then go in the amusements, but not the same place they'd gone in, wait to see where they were, and, as they were looking round, I'd go up to them and say;

"Are you winning?"

After that there'd be giggles, I'd chat the girl up, we'd get our photo taken, have our kiss, and then I'd say, 'I've got to go now but write down your address'. And then I'd be off and on to the next girl to do it again.

At the end of the night we'd have a stack of photos. One I even had up until ten years ago, I remember the address still, even what she was wearing. She was nice. I do have a selective memory and did always have a knack of remembering numbers, which helped. One girl, Elaine, stuck in my mind, (she had massive boobs which helped), and I still remembered her number, and even her address, 40 years later (although by the time I got around to trying her number it was long gone).

That time in Scarborough, the pulling, the attention, was a fantastic thing for me because it was like freedom. Everywhere I went I had this in-built understanding that, deep down, I was, at least in some ways, attractive to other people.

Whether that was my personality, my looks or a combination of both, I don't know. I guess at that age you don't really question stuff like that. I was just always amazed when it paid off for me. Years later, when I started having real mental issues, I used to hide behind that young person mask and pretend he was still with me.

After school, the very first job I had was at Davis of Bond Street, an old school department store, very much like *Are You Being Served*, with different departments. My department was menswear and my boss was Herbert, about 60 years old, tape measure slung round his neck for inner leg measurements and all that malarkey.

I started there prior to Christmas and the tradition at Davis' was that you went to every department, and every department had drinks in, so you got drinks and a Christmas kiss. So, I got quite considerably drunk, as you'd imagine.

Anyway, a girl from the ladies' department came to see me and things got heated. We had a cutting room at the back of the menswear department, and I took her in there and had her on the bench. As we were messing about I heard a voice call my name. Now I thought it was the warehouse lad, so I shouted back.

"Wait your fucking turn!"

But it was the Store Manager.

"Get in my office now!"

And of course, I was binned there and then.

I had to tell my Mum and Dad that it was a part time job and had ended. But that was my first taste of full-time employment.

After that I had my first proper, permanent job, at a furniture shop, Castles of Mayfair, run by Mr Gerald and Mr Paul (their first names, not their last names, a common Jewish propensity at the time). My Dad took me to the interview, and I was asked by the Store Manager, if I was anti-Semitic. Dad answered for me, saying 'He doesn't know what that means but no, he's not'.

Mr Gerald and Mr Paul insisted we use their forenames after Mr, but I always felt there was something very demeaning about it, almost subservient. I've never been one to eat humble pie and even at that age I refused to do it. If I needed to get their attention, I'd just say, 'Excuse me' and leave off the 'Mr' and the name.

The shop itself used to be a jeep station for US troops but now it was one of those dusty old furniture shops that sold high quality furniture that nobody could afford.

The manager had haemorrhoids and used to make me go and get him his haemorrhoid cream from the chemists. The girls behind the counter always used to giggle, asking 'Is this for you?'

'No. It's for my boss.' I always shrugged, not knowing what I was buying for him.

It was one of those jobs where, at the end of the week, the owner would come around to everyone and hand them their pay in an envelope, expecting a 'Thank you Mr Gerald' in response.

That Christmas, Mr Gerald and Mr Paul lined up all their employees and went to each one in turn to give them something for Christmas.

The senior salesman, John, was a lovely guy, a big guy with a slightly gimpy foot and he used to walk with a limp, leaning over to one side. Mr Gerald went up to him, with one of his lackeys carrying a big turkey and a bottle of what was clearly decent quality wine.

"Merry Christmas John." Mr Gerald said, as the gifts were handed over and I swear John was almost tugging at his forelock and doing his best to bow to him. Then he came to me.

"Merry Christmas Stephen," he said, his lackey handing over a chicken which, after looking at the turkey he'd given John, looked more like Tweety Pie. It was about the size of a quail.

'Oh,' I thought, 'Is that it?' "Er... thank you." I mumbled.

And then Mr Gerald handed me a bottle of wine which was the wine equivalent of Rola Cola.

I probably didn't hide my disappointment very well. As Mr Gerald left, John turned to me.

"Do you know, I've been here forty years," he said, in all seriousness, filled with pride, "When you've been here forty years, *you'll* get a turkey."

That frightened the life out of me.

Suddenly everything came into perspective. It was like a scene in a film where the walls start closing in and everything shrinks in around the camera.

I didn't want that to be me for the next forty years.

I had to get out.

A few weeks after, during my dinner break from the furniture shop, I was walking around town and walked past the recruiting office for the Air force and Navy. I was already looking for escape routes by then, so it got my attention. As I looked through the window I saw behind the desk of the Air force office this gorgeous young WAAF.

I took this as a cue. 'Come on then' I said to myself and forced myself to walk in.

"Can I help you?" she smiled.

"Yeah, yeah," I answered with youthful enthusiasm, "I want to be a pilot."

"Oh right," she sounded less enthusiastic, "What's your school results?"

Now I've always been economical with the facts about my school results, I don't know why, probably embarrassed I didn't do better. But I told the truth then.

"No, no," she shook her head, "You'll never be a pilot with that. Why don't you try the Navy?"

So, I did.

I went across to the other side of the office. Behind the Navy desk was an old Chief Petty Officer. He looked about 3 days older than God to me.

"Can I help you son?"

"Yeah, I want to join up."

He didn't ask for my school results or anything else. There and then I went upstairs and took a test, the medical was a week later and I was in.

At the interview I was asked what I wanted to do on ship.

"Er...." I had no idea. Why would I? I'd never been to sea.

The guy nodded at that response.

"Seaman." he said firmly.

"Oh, right…" it didn't sound that exciting.
"But you could sub-branch" he said encouragingly, "Radar?"
"Yeah!"
"There we are then. Seaman Operator: Radar."

And that was me. My documents say, qualified for the Navy 13.4.76.

Finally, I was escaping. But little did I know I needed my parents' signature. I was only sixteen, not old enough to sign up without their permission.

Mum was sat in the dining room when I dropped all my paperwork in front of her.

"What do you want to sign up for?" she asked, "Don't you like it round here?"

What do you say? Of course, I didn't.

I can't remember how I answered. I just said I wanted to join up.

"You'll need your real mum's signature," Dad said, as if that might talk me out of it.

"Alright." I shrugged, not fazed at all. I knew what I was going to do by now.

When I spoke to my real mum on the phone she tried to get my Dad to bring me down to Scunthorpe as well.

"Get your Dad to come around for a cup of tea," she said.

I got the feeling that she really wanted to see my dad again, despite the fact it was her that did the dirty on him! Can't say I blame her – he was a tall, handsome guy.

But Dad's like me.

"No chance." Was all he said to the suggestion of seeing her.

I got the impression that she was dead to him. She'd done the dirty and he wasn't the kind of guy that dealt well with that kind of thing, like me, and he'd rather cut her off dead. No second chances.

Later, after the papers were all signed, the receptionist at the furniture shop, who I hardly ever dealt with, because she was in the other office, took me aside.

"I heard you're joining the Navy," she said, "Let me give you something to remember me by when you go."

And then she leaned in and gave me a kiss. Like, a *proper* kiss. I wasn't a virgin at that point, but she was a grown woman!

And then she handed me a photograph. And the photograph was of her. Naked.

I gave her a look, like 'where did this come from'?

"So, you can show all the sailors on the ship," she said, "I used to be a Mayfair model." It looked like it too; it was a proper professional photo.

If I knew then what I know now, looking back, I can only think what a missed opportunity that was. She might have let me do it – but I was young and dumb. Right then, at that age, I was like a rabbit caught in the headlights.

I had that photo of hers for years but, because it was that professional, nobody ever believed me that she'd given it to me.

"She gave this to me!"
"She never!"
"It's a photo of her!"
"As if!"
"She kissed me!"
"Fuck off!"

In the Navy

There was a leaving party for me, just before I shipped off, at the pub I grew up in, although I felt it was more for everybody else than me. I remember being the happiest one there. It was as if I was being made to feel guilty for wanting to get away. My Aunty came up to me and said;
"Why do you look so pleased? You're leaving tomorrow."
And all I thought was, "Fucking yeah!" I was over the moon.
Looking around me, all I could think was, 'I'm actually escaping and you're not. And what's worse, you all have the choice to escape but you don't.'
On the odd occasion when I used to go back, even years and years later, if I ever went in the pub and saw someone I knew I'd think, 'You've sat in that seat, you've come in that pub for the last thirty years...?' and to me that felt like a prison sentence.
To them it was their life. And I know we are all different. But I always felt grateful to be going away and going to different places and wherever I laid my hat that was my home. I was comfortable with that. I felt as comfortable in a stranger's house as I would in my own bedroom.
At the station the next morning, as my Mum and Dad came to see me off, there were no tears, but I could tell they were getting a bit emotional.
As the train pulled away, I stuck my head out the window for the requisite amount of time I could get away with, which was about 30 seconds and then didn't speak to them again for nine weeks. And when I did, I rang to see how the dog was.
My Mum was furious.
"Do you know how long it's been?"
"No. How's Fred?"
"*Fred*?! It's been nine weeks!"

I genuinely hadn't kept track of time or thought to call before. I only did because I missed the dog and I wanted to let them know how much I was enjoying my independence. With hindsight it seems a tad selfish – but hindsight's a wonderful thing isn't it?

It was a surprise to me when Mum told me it had been nine weeks, but it didn't faze me. I just thought '…and…?' I was probably really thinking 'Surely you're not bothered about not hearing from me? Why are you making a scene? And no, I'm not coming home for Christmas'. I probably only went back for Christmas once in my whole naval career.

On that train journey down to basic training at HMS Raleigh, I had to change at Birmingham. Waiting to change trains at Birmingham I met another guy who was joining up. We were both sat with nothing to do, so I turned to him;

"Fancy a drink?"

"Go on then!"

So, we sat in the buffet looking out at the station and the trains coming and going, drinking multiple cans of beer. After sinking four or five we watched a train go by.

I turned to him with a grin and said, "Do you know…Wouldn't it be fucking funny if that was our train?"

And, of course, it was.

So, we turned up at the Tor Point ferry, which was long closed, at half ten at night.

"Where're you lads going?"

"HMS Raleigh!"

"Fucking hell! Not now you're not! We'll have to give 'em a bell and see what they can do for you."

They had to send some sort of dinghy out for us in the end. First day in the Navy and I turned up late. And drunk. A portend of things to come…

It didn't make for a great first impression, but it was easily forgotten. We were basically still civilians at that stage; we could PVR (pre-voluntary release) at any time up to about fourteen weeks if we thought we'd had enough.

That was before any of the indoctrination started, but that only takes three or four months for that to take hold. For me it was still all an adventure.

So basic training began, I was in Anson 26 class and my training officer was Chief Petty Officer Moth, 'Tiger' Moth to us newbie's. He was a little guy with a cap over his eyes and a swagger stick, just like Full Metal Jacket, and I found him incredibly funny.

Training was on land and sea at Raleigh and Tor Point, which was just over the water from Plymouth. As much as it was nearby major towns and populations, you were kept very separate from civilisation. After nine weeks of training, despite the bromide we knew they put in our tea to stop our sexual urges, as we were all red-blooded young men, we were all gagging to get out and get off base.

The process to get out was named the Liberty Ship. Everything in the Navy is named as if it was at sea, even when it's not.

A week before we were due to get out we had a regular kit inspection from Tiger Moth. Now these are tough. The inspection takes about ten minutes per person, nearly everything's got to be folded to the same size as your Navy manual, which is just unbelievable - you've never seen anything like it.

Tiger Moth liked the underside of your boots to be polished, like glass, which was his thing. We all knew this, but I've never been able to polish boots, underside or over, I just can't do it. I normally used to get somebody else to help but on this occasion the underside got missed.

We were all stood to attention waiting while Tiger Moth went from kit to kit. It was June of 1976, hottest summer on record at the time, so all the windows were open, and we were all sweating like thieves.

Tiger moth came up to my kit and, he must have been psychic, because he went straight to my boots.

"What the fuck's that?!" he said.

"It's a pair of boots Sir."

"Don't get fucking funny with me! What the fuck's under there?"

"I don't know what you're asking Sir…?" I mean, they were clean; you could eat your dinner off them, but clearly not good enough for him.

"I'm asking why it's not polished underneath your boots! You could -" he then said some expletives and adjective along the lines of likening the underside of my boots with a coal miners' arse. He was shouting this in a shrill 'I can't *beeeelieeve* this is happening' kind of voice – and despite his near apoplexy, I could feel myself starting to go.

Then he got my bed and tipped it up, all over the floor. But not before grabbing my boots and throwing them out the window.

I found this incredibly funny. I just burst out laughing while everyone else was wide eyed with horror.

"Stand up!" Tiger Moth started yelling, I mean, really screaming, while I was doubled up, crying with laughter, "What's wrong with you?!"

"My boots!" I could hardly speak for laughing, "You threw my boots out the window…"

Then everybody else started going and Tiger Moth started losing it, stamping up and down, this tiny little bloke in his peaked cap.

"Get downstairs to my office! Get fucking downstairs to my office!"

I went downstairs and stood outside his door as he went inside. Then he came out and stood in front of me, looking at me. He knew what he was doing, he had a little smirk on his face, not a nasty smirk, and I couldn't help it. I laughed again.

He went back in his office. Fifteen minutes later he comes out, looks at me and the process repeats again as I crack up laughing. I was there for about four hours in the end.

At this point he invites me into his office. So, I go into the office and there's a big board by the side of his desk which was filled with what I later learned were station cards.

"I'm going to give you one last opportunity to stop laughing."

"Right, ok sir."

"If you can stop laughing for maybe five seconds, we'll call it a day. Because I'm tired and I'm fucking sure you are."

"Right sir…right…."

So, I stood there, looking at him, with his little cap on…and I went. About four times. I absolutely couldn't help it.

"Right," he said, taking a bit of paper in his hands and tearing it up, "Do you know what that was?"

"No."

"That's your station card. You ain't going anywhere. Not for another four weeks."

I stopped then.

"You're not laughing now, are you?" he said.

And I wasn't. I felt murderous. It's incredible how quickly you can change. I might be embellishing with hindsight but I'm pretty sure I was looking round the office for things to attack him with.

I instantly started stammering. I still stammer sometimes when I'm under pressure.

"You m-m-mean…y-you…you mean I-I-I can't…."

"You're going nowhere. The Liberty Ship sails without you."

And everybody left without me. It was another four weeks before I got into Torpoint town centre.

But even after that, I still got on with him. I always got on with everyone. I was tolerant with some things and intolerant with others.

Overall I quite enjoyed the order and the routine that the Navy brought. I thrived in that atmosphere. I was very fit and capable, and I had always been not unintelligent, maybe not academically, but I always grasped everything.

For some reason I had managed to escape the barber and still had my luscious locks while everyone else had a "boule a zero", and it was really narking the other trainees.

I finally got called and sat down in front of the barber who seemed to have ideas above his station, thinking he was an actual hairdresser.

"Right then, young 'un. How would you like it?" he said, clapping his hands together. I don't remember what I said but it was something along the lines of, "Everyone who's come out of here has had it the same way. Get it lopped off!"

So, he did. BUZZ; gone. He made a right mess of it as well.

We were all sprogs then, baby sailors. It seems you're a sprog till you've done twenty years sometimes. On my first run out at Torpoint

I ran into some US Marine Corps. They made me feel like a baby sailor. I was 5'7" and 140 lbs dripping wet and the guy opposite me was the same age as me and was a *mountain*.

They all had skin heads, massive biceps and IDs with *US Marine Corps* on. They were proper. Fucking brilliant.

I joined the Navy because I didn't want to fight, I wanted to travel the world and meet loads of people and sleep with them, which is what I tried to do back then, and I didn't want anybody to shoot at me. The marines were hard core, fresh from boot camp, proper gung-ho and that really stuck with me.

As I said, it was the summer of '76 when I was training, and it was hot. There were several people fainting on the parade ground.

When they did, they were deliberately dragged off by their arms, so their boots dragged along the ground, leaving tramlines on the parade ground, ruining weeks' worth of hard work in polishing them. You were told if you fainted your boots were fucked.

'If you want to be sick, go down on one knee, be sick in your cap and stand up.' They told you. But don't faint. I used to tense the muscle groups in my body one by one, just to keep from cramping up. If you were the first class on the parade ground, you could be stood still for up to a couple of hours.

Appearances are important in the Navy. It's an important part of naval training to think that 'a clean ship is a fighting ship' and I still carry that ethos today. Blimey, it took me about five years before I stopped tucking my laces into my shoes when I took 'em off.

The Navy teach you how to wash yourself, how to dry yourself properly, to clean your shoes, how to iron your kit. The ironing was a fucking nightmare. Back then it was seven creases down your trousers to represent the seven oceans; inverted, external, inverted, external... Now it's all polyester so there's none of that, but then it was serge, and you had to iron it in by hand, all at different levels.

The Navy also teaches you to hate crabs. A crab is a dirty sailor, a sailor who doesn't look after his kit properly, doesn't keep himself clean and puts the rest of his shipmates to shame. In one of my class photos, there's about thirty guys there all in whites and there's just one guy in the middle who's got a big stain in the middle of his whites and he stands out a mile. He got binned in the end, because he couldn't keep himself clean.

And if you get a crab in your room, they get beasted, just like in the films, A Few Good Men and the like, top and tail tying them into their bed and then beasting. They get treated very harshly. I never took part in any of that, I didn't have the heart to, but I knew it went on.

As part of our training, they put three of us in a 26-foot Hurley sailing boat. It had a couple of sails and a tiny 'putt putt' motor and they sent us to Cowes for the boating weekend, sailing from Torpoint to Cowes.

They train you to read the sea maps, so you know what you're doing but still, we were only teenagers left to go off and do it on our own.

We had a marvellous time in Cowes but on the way back we hit a gale.

I'm not exaggerating; it was probably a force 8 or 9 ripper. You couldn't see ten foot off the sides, and we had to tie ourselves to the boat. One of us was tied to the tiller, the sails were down, so another guy was tied to the mast and I was tied to the front. I imagine I looked like a weathered mad sea captain astride the bridge of his ship.

I remember us laughing like demons, no fear at all, as we flew out of the storm, hurtling out like in the movies onto suddenly becalmed waters. How we survived, I have no idea. The waves must have been thirty foot. It was that bad they'd stopped the Torpoint ferry, and that was inland.

Even at the time I remember thinking 'We're just 16/17 and we've just sailed a ship to Cowes and back, through a storm. That's incredible!''. It does give you a sense of self-worth.

In training during the day, we had classroom lessons where we were shown pictures of Russian ships and Russian aircraft with the message, 'this is the enemy', because it was the Cold War then, and that was how you were geared to think.

I went to HMS Dryad for my subset training in radar, a land-based training unit, not an actual ship. This was weeks and weeks of manual training, learning how to use chinagraph plotting. If you've seen the films with all these people plotting out radar paths, drawing back to front on these huge glass screens, that's exactly what I was doing.

I didn't have much time off base at HMS Dryad. The days were always ordered and structured and you were busy all the time and tired. One thing I did find time for, though, when I first joined up, was a boxing trial, which I'll come back to later.

After training was just about finished, we were all gathered together for our chance to pick a ship or choose one from the list given you. The ships are called out and we put our hands up for whichever we like the sound of. The caller then reads out the pink slip which contains the ship's itinerary, so we learn where we're going and what we'll be doing for the next few months at sea.

So, the guy at the front reads out "HMS Birmingham". I had no idea what that was, but it would turn out to be, alongside HMS Sheffield, one of a new type of class 42 Destroyer.

"It's brand new," he continued, "So it's going to go to Portland work-up. Sea trials. Lots and lots of hard work."

"Go on then," I put my hand up, not knowing anything about the Birmingham other than what he'd just told me.

Then he gets the pink slip.

"And the pink slip," he continued, "After Portland work-up, you're going to the Americas for nine months. East and West Coast."

The whole room erupted. 'Get in!' 'Fucking America! Yes!'

"There's only one thing," he said, "It's been fitted with ADAWS computerised weapons system. So, your nine weeks of chinagraphing mean doodly squat. You're going to have to do another ten weeks of computer training."

Not that we had any choice in the matter, but it was alright with me, a worthwhile trade-off for that itinerary. And, I would turn out to have a real knack for the computerised system.

I joined the Birmingham end of 1976, just before Christmas. It was the first ship I'd ever been on and it really was a beautiful ship.

I took my kit on board and headed straight for the RP's mess. The Birmingham was a single prop ship, one huge screw propeller, and the RP's mess was just on top of that. As you'd expect the noise was incredible, but you get used to it. Even now I've got a midi file with ships' propeller sounds on it to help me off to sleep, and I don't sleep well at all. But that sound helps.

The first person I saw when I got to the mess was a guy called Whisky Walker. Whisky Walker had been a Leading Hand, down to Able Seaman, up to Petty Officer, then to Leading Hand, up the ranks and down and then up again...

He was an alcoholic. There were quite a lot of them in the Navy. Maybe not so much now. Like a lot of people, he looked old to me, craggy.

Back then, new on the ship, I announced myself.

"Hi, I'm Steve Utting; I'm joining in January, after the New Year. Where can I put my kit bag?"

Whisky Walker pointed at the ground.

"Yeah, leave it there."

"In the open you mean?"

"Yeah." he nodded, looking at me as if I was an idiot as I hesitated, "It'll be there when you come back." And then he fucked off.

And he was right. You can leave anything out anywhere on a ship. Because, if you find a thief in the Navy, the punishments are harsh, from your colleagues that is. You can leave your locker open, day or night.

"Can I borrow some fags?"

"In my locker!"

"Can I borrow twenty quid?"

"In my locker!"

You have to be like that, open and honest and with nothing to fear from thieves.

I didn't go home for Christmas, as I knew I wouldn't, staying with some girl in Portsmouth. Then I joined the ship in the New Year, finding my kit bag where I left it.

My first shower when I joined the ship was an experience. I was still young, not even shaving and a bit hesitant when I asked where I should go.

Ollie, a young sailor who looked about ten, when he was about 27, and who was also a bit camp, piped up;
"Ooh, I'll take you."
"No, you're alright, just show me where they are."

"No, I'll take you," he says, "Let me just get me flip flops on."
Now there's a myth that surrounds gay sailors. These days' gay and lesbian citizens can serve openly in the forces and have been since 2000. Prior to that it was very different. If someone was 'found', and they were found, to be gay, then they were binned. Simple as that.
But still I wasn't sure about Ollie taking me to the shower.
"Come on," he says.
"Fuck off!"
And now everybody starts joining in, getting in on the joke.
"Go on! Go and get your fucking shower!"
"I'm not going with him! He wants to hold my hand!"
I went with Ollie in the end and nothing happened. He probably made a few comments about the size of my knob, but that sort of thing's typical Navy humour. The Navy is made up of some real characters. Some are married, in it for the career, some in it for the adventure, some are Lotharios, like me, and in it for that. But if you can't take a joke in the Navy, you're in the wrong place.
You'll get things like the guy with the biggest knob in the mess coming up behind you resting his meat and two veg on your shoulder while you're watching telly.
"Fucking hell! Charlie!"
Charlie Brown was his name, being smooth was his game and that was his party trick. He was a right womanizer as well. But he'd act all innocent.
"What? What's up with you? Haven't you ever seen one before?"
Once he'd done it once he'd never do it again and it never happens outside of the ship because you're not in that sort of environment. But those sorts of jokes were common currency on ship.
One was 'helicopter exercise'. You'd be resting in the bunk and someone would shout "Helicopter exercise! Steve! Get the lights!" And you'd jump out of bed to switch off the lights before realising

that the mess is two floors down and there's no way a helicopter's going to see the light from it.

"You fuckers!"

Like I said, you need to be able to take a joke. And there were loads more.

Like the long wait, when you're a lad, you've never heard of that but in the Navy, you'll also be asked to get the spare lash, as you're coming into dock. Now a lash is a piece of rope, so that makes sense. A spare lash, an extra lash, seems reasonable.

So, you go up on deck to ask for the spare lash.

"Ok, wait there."

And you'll stand waiting as the anchor goes down with a splash.

"There you go."

"What?!"

But that was it. The spare lash. 'Sper-lash'.

I was responsible for a joke of my own, one that got totally out of hand, a thing called the parrot. Obviously, parrots are something that's synonymous with the Navy. And what do parrots do? Parrots repeat.

What I'd do is I'd be speaking to somebody and then pretend I hadn't heard something, so they repeat it. As soon as they did I'd make a 'swoosh' noise and point at my shoulder, to say 'Get on my shoulder. You're a parrot'.

Now this started to spread around the whole ship like wildfire, to the point that people were getting paranoid about repeating anything, even when asked. So, you'd be asking ten or twelve times, swearing on your Mother's life that you never heard them the first time and that you wouldn't do the parrot.

"I promise! I promise! I never heard you!" Oscar worthy acting, "I never heard you! I won't do it!"

And as soon as they repeated themselves.

Swoosh. Get on my shoulder.

On the bird theme I also started a craze, all over the ship, for doing the funky chicken.

I was reading a book called The Choirboys by Joseph Wambaugh, all about the night section of the Los Angeles police department and all the characters there. One of these cops was called Roscoe and he used to make any perps that wouldn't go quietly do 'the funky chicken' by doing a chokehold on them. And it described how to do this chokehold in the book.

You can do it, with the same effect, voluntarily. If you bend down on your haunches, with your head down, take a deep breath, stand up, deep breath, and bend down then with your last deep breath hold, with your arms out. Then somebody comes around and crushes your chest and just as you're about to pass out, they let go. And then you pass out.

When you come to it's like you're waking up in an alien world. Your mind doesn't know where it is yet. I remember waking up and seeing feet and wondering what they were. Incredible feeling. And then when you come out of that, you do the funky chicken, as your body goes into spasm as it comes back to life.

We started out doing it as a dare, daring everybody to do it voluntarily. And then when they didn't, we used to go around in gangs, not just us as well, choke holding them. You'd go to the back of the dinner queue, for instance, and grab someone and chokehold them. Somebody would be in front and as soon as your victim's eyes went, they'd tell you and you'd let them drop.

It was all around the ship; people were dropping like flies. I think of it now and just think how did we get away with it? Why did it happen?

In the end the Skipper had to put out a message saying it had to stop as it was dangerous, so that put an end to it.

But nothing beat the joke played on me by the whole ship.

Early in deployment, while we'd been at sea a fair while, I was walking down the middle of the ship's drag (main walkway) and saw a notice saying:

Wanted: Person of sound nature – looking for adventure

Splash Target Coxswain

Incredibly dangerous job. Put your name down below.

There were about ten names there, so I thought I'd put my name down too.

Now this was all contrived, the whole ship was in on this. It's done once every four or five years, maybe. Any more often than that and it wouldn't work. I've tried to find that copy of the Naval News with the photo in it online but that copy's missing.

So over the next three or four weeks I was called to the doctor's bay and started having regular tests, blood tests, exercise, powers of recovery, vision, they had me wearing different kinds of uniforms, snorkels, all that sort of stuff, and I didn't question any of it, I was just really caught up in the moment.

The day comes and I get ready to go out on deck, I've got on anti-flash gear (in case of nuclear explosions); white cloth cap and goggles, I've got full emergency gear on, uniform, flippers, air tanks on my back, gas mask, I've got everything. It probably weighed about a ton.

I got on deck and the quarter deck was rammed, with a splash target sat in the middle of everyone. Even then, even then, I didn't twig.

The splash target is a lattice of wood with a kind of reversed postman chute on top, attached to about 80 fathoms of multi-plait rope. It's towed behind the ship and the funnel at the front kicks out a splash that Royal Navy Canberra aircraft use as target practise for strafing runs, with aircraft cannons. On top of this splash target was a chair and in front of it was a rope, like a barrier on a waltzer, for me to grab onto.

The Captain came up to me, camera flashes going off everywhere.
"Right Utting. Are ready?"
"Yes sir. Ready. Ready."
"Strapped in?"
"Yes sir. Strapped in."
"Remembered all the signals?"
"Signals. Yes sir."

Now I'm not paying attention to anything but the Captain. I'm all goggled up and oblivious to the flash bulbs going off or any banter and hilarity.

"We're just going to run through a few now," he said, "Cannon fire to the right."
I put my right arm up.
"Cannon fire to the left."
I put my left arms up.
"Cannon fire on target."
"I crossed my arms."
"Perfect!" the Captain grinned, handing me a certificate.

The Certificate was a big long thing, saying "This rating, being of sound mind and body…" carrying on along on those sorts of long and wordy lines and ending with "But above all this rating has a sense of humour second to none, signed Captain J Symonds".

And then I said the immortal words, "Can you hold it until I get back, Sir?"

He just smiled.

"You're not going anywhere lad," he said, "Let's put the target out and see what comes back."

Of course, what came back were a few bits of shredded wood.

Even though the whole ship was in on it, I never felt any resentment. There was no nastiness to it, no viciousness, nobody teased me about it. Splash target coxswains are few and far between, or otherwise it wouldn't work, so it was special to get to be one.

After work-up the Birmingham headed north for cold weather trials.

The cold weather trials were the longest time I've ever been at sea without hitting port, two months from the time we left port to the time we got back. We went all the way up to Kodiak Island, at the top of the world.

Once you get past a certain point North, the ship is constantly under the weight of ice, so that the ships at a fifteen-degree stern down position, always, just due to the ice weighing it down.

To combat that, you have ice chipping parties that work twenty minutes at a time. You've got thermal underwear on, your work wear on, your jumper on, your one piece survival suit, three different layers of gloves and you go up and have to unclip the guys from the last ice chipping party, because their hands are so cold, after just twenty minutes work, that they can't move them to do it themselves. Then you walk to your bit of the ship with a rubber mallet and started chipping off ice.

At the time of year, we went, around summer, it was constantly dusk. Any time of day you went up top it looked like teatime. There was no difference between the boundary of sea and sky. The sea was permanently black, with the occasional white crest, if there was breeze. It was an incredible vista, like being on the moon, I imagine. But oppressive.

It was dangerous too. We were told that if you fall overboard in those waters the ship won't stop for you, it won't turn around for you, and it won't look for you. You're gone. If you fall overboard in your full body suit, you'll survive about two minutes. Without it you're dead soon as you hit that water.

It was that cold you'd throw a bucket of water onto the deck and it would be frozen in seconds... So of course, you'd all dare each other to be out on deck in minus thirty degrees in your skivvies, before locking the door on them.

"Don't fall overboard! We're not stopping!"

Because it was the Cold War, the whole time we were North of whatever point it was, there were Russian Badger Delta aircraft, Soviet planes with sonar/radar discs on top, circling at five miles or less of the ship, at all times, to keep track of what we were up to.

We were told *never* to go up to take photos of these aircraft. Somebody put the word around that there was a Badger Delta visible; close enough to see the red stars on its wing tips. Within a minute the order came from the bridge, 'do not photograph the plane'. So of course, everybody rushes on deck with their cameras to take photos of this mysterious jet-black aircraft flying around.

The skipper decided to go into an ice float, to see if the ship could take it. As a result, he pranged the sonar, the bulb underneath the bow of the ship, which had to get fixed when we were next in dry dock. I don't know what sort of reprimand he must have got for that -

he'll have got something, but we were all impressed that he'd even tried.

Of course, two months at sea is a long time. After the sea trials, we were all gagging to get back to port to get back to real life. And my life in port was more exciting than most.

On the Town

Back in the day pub opening times were night times until 11. It was unheard of for a pub to be open during the day. The earliest opening pub in Portsmouth was the Home Club, which was a sailor's only club, which opened at 4.30.

What I used to do, after finishing my duties, was 'shit, shower, shave n shampoo' then straight to the Home Club. Then it would be on to The Mighty Fine, from there to the City Arms and then on to the Bistro club to finish. Now and then I would take in some different pubs on the way, but I had my favourites. Bear in mind I was young then and my capacity for drinking was huge.

The Mighty Fine is on the Portsmouth old pubs website with the tagline;

"The Mighty Fine – not so mighty, not so fine.

One of Portsmouth's most notorious drinking establishments"

It had no windows; it was dark and dingy, and I LOVED it.

The City Arms was also one of those sorts of places you wouldn't really be safe if you weren't a local, an Irish pub, but I knew a lot of locals. I never cultivated that, I just seemed to get on with folk, kept myself to myself and didn't really present a threat.

In the Mighty Fine I knew everyone, and I slept with all the barmaids too. One of the barmaids, Lorna, was known as rubber-legs Lorna, because the legend was that she could put her legs behind her head. Which, of course, she could.

I never had enemies, no bitterness, no jealousy, I'd sleep with Lorna one week and the next week I'd sleep with Erica. It also meant of course, that I never waited long to be served and I got no slops. Winner winner.

When I was on a weekend sesh the landlord of The Mighty Fine used to let me stay over for the night, sleeping in the bar. Well, I was one of his best customers (and I also kept his barmaids happy).

I'd always glass collect at the end of the night just to be useful. It would have felt wrong not to, while I was there, since he was letting me stay the night.

The Mighty Fine always felt like home as soon as I walked in, taking a dark corner and ordering a bitter top, a bitter with a top of Southern Comfort, which I'd drink down until it was just Southern Comfort.

There was one night I was at the Mighty Fine, feeling at home as ever, and I was just heading over to the serving hatch to get some chips. On the way this girl came up to me.

"Are you Steve?"

"Yeah."

"Steve from the ship?"

"Yeah yeah."

"I'm a student, I've just come down from Leeds for the weekend to stay with my friend," she said, "She says you're a good shag. How about proving it to me?"

Now to explain my answer, you'll need to realise how often this sort of thing happened back then, and how regular my schedule was.

"I will..." I said tentatively, "But I do go to Bistros, every night. And I'm going to Bistros tonight. So... if it's going to happen, we'll need to go in the next hour or so. Where's your mate's flat?"

She told me and, as it happens, it was on the way to Bistros.

We went back to the flat and, as we got in, I shagged her in the hallway, then I shagged her on the stairs and then I shagged her in the shower. Then, I headed off to Bistros and left her to stay with her friend. Unbelievable.

(Note – I have read that last anecdote back several times since I wrote it and no matter how I try, I *can't* put it any other way. You are just going to have to take my word for it.)

The Bistro Club was in the Portsmouth tourist guide, but it was a bit of a joke. I'm sure when it was first built it was different – maybe not. Sailors never used to go there; it had a terrible reputation and was quite dangerous. But what they always did do was play a joke on all the new sailors, telling them about this great place in Portsmouth, that you'd have to wear your best bib and tucker for, that they'd then take you to and then leave you and see how you cope.

So, they took me, best bib and tucker and all, to a place most sailors ran from, and I loved it. It was dark and always rammed. The glass collector/doorman was a dwarf guy who had a knife in his boot and took no shit from no one. It was perfect.

After not very long at all, the others were all; "We're leaving you now Steve" and I was "Yeah yeah, see ya!", and stayed there all night. I loved it.

The dance floor was up a set of nearly vertical stairs, plastic glasses, no tables, DJ behind a plexi-glass shield. But it was always packed, and the music was amazing.

Behind the bar was this enormous black woman who I got to calling Mama Kath, who absolutely loved me and always looked after me. If ever I was out of money she'd give me beer, if I was out of fags she'd give me fags. Always looked after me. Lovely woman.

I made it my home. I always used to end the night at Bistros. There was a membership card and not many people had one, maybe because of the initiation. But I made myself a member.

The initiation ceremony for membership of Bistros was called the flying angel. The aim was to take two pints of beer, one in each hand, and launch yourself down the stairs and all the locals, including Yorkie C, who we'll meet in a bit, catch you at the bottom.

"I want a membership card!" I announced one evening. Of course, I knew what I had to do for it.

"Go on Steve! Do it!"

To pass the test you must still have the pint glasses in your hands when you get to the bottom. Which, obviously, I did.

Coincidentally, the flying angel is the name of a field gunner role. The flying angel is usually the smallest field gunner who goes down with the gun barrel. He's the smallest because it's less drag on the zip wire. I had quite an altercation with some Field Gunners – but more of that later.

One of my regular girlfriends, who I'd met at Bistros, was Big Shaz.

We had a relationship where, if I didn't have anywhere else to go or just fancied it, I could always go back to her flat at Nightingale Road. This was located just across the road from Bistro's.

She never seemed to have anyone else there, not that she was unattractive, maybe it was just my good luck, but she always had time for me. I'd go around there, she'd cook me food, we'd have sex and she'd cook me breakfast in the morning.

One night I was chatting with Shaz at Bistros when this woman came in trailing two huge minders.

"Who's that?" I asked.

"That's Dawn," Shaz said, "She owns the Bistro."

And of course, that was like a red rag to a bull for me. Dawn was like the Crystal Maze and the Krypton Factor rolled into one. Owner of Bistros? Now there's a challenge.

"The owner of the Bistro?!" I clapped my hands together, "Right, Shaz. Introduce me!"

"There's no fucking way -"

"Introduce me! Introduce me!"

Sharon introduced me, as asked, and me and Dawn got talking. She was maybe mid-thirties, with long dark hair and Scottish, as it turned out.

It seems arrogant but back then I had something about me, I couldn't deny it- that was attractive to women. I had that confidence about me, but I also had that vulnerability that I could turn on when needed. And that was what I used this time.

Eventually after a bit of chatting, Dawn asked if I wanted to come back to hers.

"Er...I'm not sure...." I acted bashful, "I've not done it before...."

I found this technique worked quite a lot. Especially since at that age I looked reet innocent. It was like lighting a blue touch paper for Dawn. She nodded reassuringly and whispered.

"I'll look after you."

We went back to hers, minders in tow and, when we got there, they left me in the tender care of Dawn.

We got to it and, after about five minutes, she delivered the immortal words, in her thick Scottish accent;

"You're nae fucking virgin."

We shagged all night on her big oak bed and ended up breaking it. It was an amazing night.

When I went out, I always went out alone, for several reasons. Firstly, I didn't want anyone cramping my style, secondly, I didn't want to have some drunken sailor hanging round my neck but, most importantly, I knew, one hundred percent, (barring an Act of God) that I wouldn't be going back to the ship that night.

So, I didn't take anybody out. The one time I did it all went tits up.

I knew all the locals in Portsmouth and for someone, in a naval town, who went out and shagged all their women; it was amazing that they all got one with me. But they did. I wasn't any trouble to anybody, and I could go in any pub, and I did go in some notorious pubs, and I was safe and sound. I used to shag the barmaids, I used to shag anybody, but I never seemed to have any trouble.

This one time a sailor I'll call Jeff, begged me to let him come to Bistros with me. Eventually I caved in and let him come along but I set him straight when we got there.

"Right," I said, "We're going upstairs, no tables, plastic glasses, blah, blah, blah. Don't look anybody in the eye. Don't say anything to anybody and don't pull anybody unless you ask me first, because I know everybody. Right? Because once we're in there, I'm gone."

"Yeah, yeah, yeah!" He was desperate enough to be let in to agree to anything.

We went up and, no lie, it must have been at most about five minutes before I heard a voice.

"Steve! Steve!" it was Jeff screaming for me.

I turned around and saw Yorkie C, a huge guy in dungarees, which was the fashion at the time, holding him up against the wall, by the neck, feet dangling above the floor.

"Steve," Yorkie C turned to me, "Is this cunt with you?"

I nodded reluctantly.

"Yeah, Yorkie, he is."

"Get him out," Yorkie said, "Or I'll pan the fucker."

"Ok Yorkie."

Yorkie dropped him and Jeff turned to me and asked me to see him out of Bistros and elsewhere to carry on our night.

"You must be dreaming," I shook my head, "If you think I'm leaving this club with you. Fuck off."

This got back to the mess soon enough, earning me a bit of a reputation for being a loner and aloof. But I'd warned him.

That was the only time I took anyone else out with me. The rest of the time I went out usually alone and there was never any trouble because I could look after myself.

All the taxi drivers used to know me. Every now and then I'd sell a watch if I was a bit short. Tailors used to come to the ship's side in travelling vans to sell all the latest fashions, as well as watches. I used to buy the 70s Suede head fashions amongst other things - the check coats, the pressed trousers. I had money to burn back then.

On the odd occasion I ran out I'd sell a watch to a taxi driver, fifty quid for a watch that cost me a hundred. And that fifty would last me a weekend.

When we were in port the Navy was the last thing on my mind. As soon as I hit the bottom of that gang plank, and nine times out of ten I went back on time, my focus was just on going out.

Part of my routine before I left ship was getting the papers and butty order from all the guys. I used to go around asking everyone because they knew I'd be out all night and I'd be coming back past the mobile chuck wagon canteens in the morning, so I'd go with a butty and paper order in my back pocket.

I never thought I was doing that as a favour, or to make people like me or because I'm a good guy. There was no thought process behind it, it was just the thing to do, as I knew I'd be out all night, and it got to be a regular thing.

Sometimes when I was on duty, I'd pay someone to take the duty for me so I could go out.

"Fucking hell! I'm on duty tomorrow! Anybody want to do a duty?"

Out of the guys in the mess there's always two or three that don't want to go out.

"Yeah, I'll do it. How much?"

"Tenner?"

And that would be it, I'd be off out for the price of ten quid. It was perfectly legal for someone else to take your duty and change the duty roster. Of course, it wasn't legal to pay them to do it, but nobody wanted to take a duty without getting something for it. And I was happy to pay a tenner to get into town. It was a lot of money back then, but it used to guarantee me getting out whenever we were in port. I probably spent more time on shore than I did on ship.

However, there was one time, in Portsmouth that I couldn't get out. I was on post on the ship's gangway, two of us guarding the ship.

A bit before eight that night I was told I had a call.

"Able Seaman Utting, telephone call, line one."

It was a girl I knew in Portsmouth, called Tina.

"Come around," she said.

"I'm on duty!" I protested.

But she made it an invitation I couldn't resist.

I went back to my opposite number on the gangplank (and looking back I just think 'why? Why in God's name...?') Knowing full well what I was about to do.

"I'm just going to get an oggy," I said, an oggy being a pasty, from the van on the dock, "Do you want one?"

"Yeah, alright," he nodded.

I went down the gangway and, without thinking about it, took off my cap and greatcoat, it was a misty, foggy night, and left them on a bollard and just went.

I got a taxi and went to Tina's, banged her and then came back, probably two or three hours later.

As I approached the ship I saw searchlights everywhere, all around the ship, as well as an ambulance and regulator (Naval police) vans and people with torches crawling all over the dock.

As I got closer I asked someone what was going on.

"Who are you?"

"Able Seaman Utting."

"Oh right," the guy turned to the search parties, "Don't worry he's here! Get the divers out; they don't need to look for him anymore!"

48

What had happened is that my oppo had started to wonder where I'd got to and had gone looking for me. Finding my coat and hat by the ship, he'd assumed I'd jumped in. Why the fuck he made that assumption, I don't know.

It was, in many ways, a funny situation but as I went back up the gangway an officer told me I would be at Captain's Table for this, obviously.

Suddenly I began to panic. Fucking hell. Captain's Table. Deserting your post. What do I do?

You get an officer, someone representing you at the table and the Lieutenant who I had was a really, super nice, decent guy. You don't find many of those, there's a big class divide in the Navy, between a rating and an officer, but he was a genuine guy. I felt, and still feel, sad for manipulating him. But I had to.

So, there I was the next day at Captain's Table facing Captain Dan Symons, and he's stood at his lectern, licking his finger as he flicks through my records.

"Do you know," he said, "When the ships at sea, I've got recommends here from officers who've worked with you in the operations room about how good you are. What is it about when the ship gets to port?"

It was something that others had repeated before and after.

"You've deserted your post," he continued, "If we were at war I'd be shooting you. You'd be shot as a deserter!"

I didn't have an answer to that. Except for the official one.

"I'd like the Lieutenant to speak for me Sir." I said.

Now I'd sold the Lieutenant a whole tale about a family of ill repute where the daughter was under incredible danger and stress and who'd rang me in a panic because someone was trying to hurt her.

The Lieutenant did an incredible job, I felt like crying myself, and he was welling up as he spoke. I was looking at the Captain and could see from his face that he was thinking 'Is this true...? Is it not...?'

"Thank you, Lieutenant," the Captain said at last.

"Alright Sir," the Lieutenant really was choking up by now, "I've said my piece."

"Well..." the Captain said, "I've never heard anything like that in my life."

'Fuck...' I thought to myself, wondering if he'd believed it, 'What am I going to get?'

I got a £140 fine, which was a lot of money in those days, and 28 days of Number Nines.

Apart from locking me up, that was the worst punishment I could have imagined.

The punishments go in numbered order. Number one is hanging at the yard arm, which you can still get for treason or arson in Her Majesty's dockyard.

Number nine is where you must report, in various uniforms, or presentation kit, to different officers, at random times of day. Because you must be available to be called on at any time, it restricts your movements, tying you 24 hours a day to be ready to receive orders to report in uniform, so you effectively can't leave the ship.

To me, at that age, it was like locking me up and throwing away the key.

"T-t-twenty eight days!" I couldn't believe it, "N-n-number nines!!"

So that was me deserting my post. It wasn't big and it wasn't clever, but it was what it was. And nine times out of ten, as I say, I made it back to the ship.

Early on I went through a punk phase, which ended up causing a change to ship's orders regarding regulation haircuts.

One of the last things my Mum said to me before I left was 'Don't get a tattoo, don't get an earring'. So, of course, the first thing I did when I was ashore was get my first tattoo and get my ear pierced.

After a little while other guys started getting their ears pierced as well, because it's allowed in the Navy, so I thought I might as well get another one. Then a few blokes on the ship got both done as well, so I went and got another one. That was when the Skipper intervened and sent down orders that no one on the ship could get any more ear piercings. That was one of two incidences where orders got sent down because of me.

During my punk phase I started getting designs cut into my hair, which was quite new at the time. Now the Navy regulations specify that you must have at least half an inch of hair, so if you fall overboard, they can grab you by the scalp and pull you in. The regulations allow you to have as much hair as you like on the top of your head, as long as it fits under your cap. We had a Jock on board called Axe-in-the-Head, because he had a mullet with a centre parting in it, because he refused to cut it, which looked like he'd had an axe in his head.

With my punk hairstyles, the diamond and zig zag patterns took the hair down to the skin so orders were sent down that nobody could get that haircut anymore.

I discovered punk just by stumbling into punks in some of the local pubs in Portsmouth, liking the look, and the music and really liking the attitude, oh, and especially the women. Punk was everywhere at the time and it felt like something you could be part of and get involved in.

I like to think I was a bit trendier than most of the punks in Portsmouth, as I used to get my gear from Mr Blues in London. Which sort of negated the point of being a punk, I suppose. I was quite a clean and tidy punk! I had a Sid Vicious leather jacket, with the white piping, that cost me three hundred quid, back then. I used to come off ship with all my punk gear in a carrier bag and get changed on the pontoon (and change back before I came back on ship).

I loved the bands, partly because of the anarchy at the gigs, because life on ship was so ordered and this was a real contrast and a release. I used to go to the Portsmouth Guildhall and for £2.50, on various nights of the week, I saw Blondie, Eddie and the Hot Rods, Nicky Tesco and the Members, Siouxsie and the Banshees, the Jam... almost too many to name.

I remember seeing Blondie, with Debbie Harry wearing a dress on stage that was all mirrors, looking just stunning. I remember seeing The Jam on their In the City tour, when they wore their black suits with red jam stripes, and they used to finish their set with the theme tune from Batman. Back then, singer-songwriters seemed few and far between, so looking at the sleeve of a Jam album and seeing 'Weller' after every track was really inspiring.

I liked the music, but I also liked the women. With hindsight I found it quite liberating, I like women that are; powerful isn't quite the right word, but those that have something about them, and the punk girls were like that. Self-assured.

Back then, I could go into any pub, any nightclub or music bar, and go into a crowd of women and come out with one. I could go up and talk to any a woman, in any crowd or group of friends, and pull. So, I'd always be able to go to one of these gigs and have a young punkette draped on my arm.

When I say I liked the punk girls, not necessarily that they were more of a challenge, but maybe they knew more what they wanted and weren't afraid to get it. One girlfriend, Rachel, very much knew what she wanted.

Rachel had a teardrop tattoo under her eye, was very physically attractive and very, very sexually forward. She was also, it turned out, bisexual.

One night I was at Rachel's flat and she asked me if I was alright to look after the flat while she went out with some friends. I wasn't really a jealous guy, so it didn't bother me. Later that night she came back, with a friend. All I thought to myself was 'Fucking hell! I'm not going to get owt tonight....'

They then got into bed with each other. I was sat there on the settee, next to the fireplace, feeling put out and then Rachel looked over to me and patted the bed.

"Come on then..."

"What....?"

"Come in here between us...." She smiled, "Show So-and-so that thing you do with your hands...."

You can imagine how the rest of the night went. Winner winner.

Before the Americas trip, and before I met Rachel, I'd got engaged. And not intentionally.

Quite a lot of civilian girls liked to catch a sailor, you got living quarters, all paid for, your husband had a good, and steady, wage. Granted they were away for months at a time, but the wives had their own cliques of military wives and all that sort of thing, so it was quite a desirable life.

I was going out with this girl, Debbie, for maybe a couple of months, if that. I was due to go out to America and my birthday would have been while I was away. Debbie told me that her parents wanted to organise a going away party for me at a club and would I come. Of course, I agreed.

When I went into the party, the hall was full of people I'd never met. At the back of the hall there was a table with a cake on it. It was a three-tiered cake. The bottom tier said, 'Happy Birthday Steve', the middle one said, 'Congratulations on your Engagement Debbie and Steve' and the top one said, 'Bon Voyage'.

I turned to Debbie in shock. This was the first I'd known. There were rings and everything.

I remember sitting on the end of a bench, on my own, because nobody there knew me, thinking, 'I don't want to get engaged!' I liked her but I didn't love her. I couldn't believe it, a cake, and a party, there were even presents!

I went away to sea and the Americas, leaving Debbie behind. There were other relationships, and plenty of sexual partners, while I was in the Americas and when I came back I met Rachel.

One day I was at Rachel's and there was a knock at the door. Rachel went and answered it and came back to me with a smug look on her face;

"There's someone here to see you," She said, clearly trying to be clever, "I think it's your fiancé?"

And then Debbie walked in, with a ring and everything. I didn't know, and don't remember now, how she found me.

"I...I just wondered when you were coming home...." She said.

I felt awful. I felt like I'd been caught out.

"I ain't..." I don't know if I said it in so many words, but it was obvious.

So, she went.

It was an awful feeling. It was embarrassing. And I felt embarrassed for me. Rachel obviously wasn't bothered. We'd both slept with other people and we were never jealous.

Really Debbie was probably the one to be with, she was a nice, ordinary girl. But Rachel was a sexual animal. Sorted.

Of the two, Rachel is the one that's really stayed with me. And for one very particular reason.

One of my things that I used to say to my girlfriends was, once I'd made the connection; "Whatever you want me to do – I'll do it."

I used to say it a lot, even at that young age of seventeen or eighteen.

"Whatever you want me to do – I'll do it."
"What do you mean?"
"Have a think – anything. I'll do it."

It was a real turn on. I found that women have just as many sexual fantasies as men - they just need releasing.

One afternoon I was with Rachel and she turned to me.
"Do you remember when you said you'd do anything?"
"Yeah?"
"Will you?"
"Yeah yeah."
"Can I tie you up?"
"Yeah, go on then."

So, she ties me up, gets on top, starts doing it and then, suddenly, stops.

"I'll be back in a minute."

She gets off, goes to the kitchen area and comes back with a knife.

"What are you doing…?"

She got back on top of me again, knife in hand, and, just by instinct, Percy jumped up, I couldn't stop him.

Rachel was one of those out there punks. Very intense. She always used to like going on top, she liked the control it gave her, looking at you while you were doing it, having that power over the situation, and I normally found it a real turn on.

But this was different.

"I'm just going to cut you," She said, "So that in years to come, whenever you look at it, you'll remember me."

I wasn't up for this.

"You'd better fucking get off me Rachel."

"I'm only going to do it the once." She said, "I swear."

And she did.

I don't know if you've heard skin ripping. It sounds a bit like sackcloth tearing. It did to me, anyhoo.

She then started licking, licking up the blood, all around the cut and around my nipples. I don't know how much of a turn on it was for her, but it wasn't for me. When she let me up, it was all I could do not to chuck her out the bloody window. I guess I asked for it though.

But she was right. Years later, whenever I looked at that little nick, although it's faded now, I thought of her. She tattooed me too, her name 'Rachel' on my shoulder, so she's always stayed with me.

Rachel was maybe an extreme example but that was the kind of life I lived when the ship was in port, it all revolved around going out and having sex.

I remember being in the Mighty Fine one time, sitting round a table with people talking about everyone else at the table's sexual prowess. There was a school of thought around the table that Yorkie C, the big guy from the Bistro, had the biggest cock, but that Steve knew what to do with his, with some saying they'd rather go with me, as I know what I'm doing.

To me, then, that all felt totally normal. And I thought it was what I wanted, the acceptance, the being wanted, no fuss, and no complications.

And that lifestyle was all that was on my mind, when the ship was in port at least.

Europe

Being in the Navy was all about seeing the world for me. I'd signed up because I wanted to see the world and meet loads of different people. And that's exactly what I did. I didn't want to fight or get shot at – so the Army was out and as I said – I couldn't be a pilot!

Europe probably wasn't the most exciting part of my naval career, but it was new and fresh.

I had one of my birthdays when we were in Jersey. The ship anchors a quarter of a mile out, because the water's too shallow to have it in port, and you get a little sailing dinghy back and forth.

The first time I went to Jersey, the very first pub I went to, I just heard this broad Scouse accent shouting;

"Alright there, Steve! How you doing? Fancy seeing you in here!"

It was one of the NAAFI girls from HMS Dryad who'd moved to Jersey for the summer and was working in the bar. This meant I never paid for a single drink the whole day. This was one of the only times I've ever drunk myself sober. I was drinking Southern Comforts and, back then, Jersey's spirit measure was a big measure, and it seemed like double ours. I sat there shooting the breeze with the NAAFI girls, got drunk and then got sober, never paying for a thing the whole time I was there.

I had a bit of history with the NAAFI girls. One of them I'd gone home with, back to her apartment on base, after a heavy night of drinking and dancing. Due to the drinking, while we were in bed, I was too drunk to get to the toilet and ended up peeing on her. We remained good friends – amazingly - and we never had sex, but the story got around the whole camp, and I got grief for it in the night, and it was funny after the event but not so much on the night. Chance missed. Bugger.

Jersey was a tax haven back then, well, it still is, but it was the sort of place you couldn't take your t-shirt off in the town centre, you couldn't get drunk and run riot. It was a place for decent minded people. We were given all that information before we went ashore for my birthday.

Normally, as I've said, I never went out with other sailors, because it used to cramp my style, and I liked my own company. I wanted to be free to pull women. But on this occasion people insisted on taking me out for my birthday.

We got on the sailing dinghy and sailed the quarter mile out to St. Helier and went out about 7 o'clock. The first pub we went to was a hotel, the George Hotel, on the seafront, out on the esplanade, with massive great plate glass windows on the front. The barman saw us coming in and you could see from the look of on his face what he thought was coming.

"Are you going to behave lads?"

"Yeah, yeah, of course we are. It's just Steve's birthday."

We started drinking and then I went for a pee. When I came back there was what we called traffic lights on the table. Everybody had bought me a short, lots of glasses, different colours and lined them up on the table.

"Go on. Drink them."

So, I knocked them back, one after the other, and obviously they went straight to my head. I went and sat at the bar, clearly the worse for wear, and someone who was sat there suggested I needed something to drink to sober me up.

"Get him a tomato juice, something like that." he said, and the tomato juice was placed on the counter.

'I don't want a tomato juice,' I said.

I grabbed the tomato juice and threw the whole lot over my shoulder and it landed, in a massive great splat, across the plate glass.

"Right. Out!" the barman was furious.

We all piled out and, as is naval tradition, the rest all went off drinking and left me.

"We're off. You're no good to us…" they headed on to another pub as I was left sitting on the step. I'd have done the same.

The rest of the details were recounted to me, as I didn't remember much at all.

I was left sat on the step and a policeman came along, took me to the harbour and put me underneath a fishing net, with my feet sticking out, so somebody could see me when the boat came in for the ship at ten or eleven o'clock.

When the boat came in somebody says, 'There's Steve's feet. Let's get him on the boat.'

On the fishing boat, down below, it was basic. Just rows of bunks on slats just above the hold. I was placed on a bottom bunk, but the sea was incredibly rough that night and, during the transit, I fell from the bottom bunk and down the three or four feet into the hold.

We got to the ship and somebody says:

"Where's Steve?!"

"Bloody hell, he's gone!"

"No, he's not, he's here."

They found me and pulled me up and then got me ready to cross back onto the ship. Below the flight deck on the battleship there's the quarter deck. Getting back on board from the fishing boat / dinghy, means removing part of the guard rail from the quarter deck and part of the guard rail on the fishing boat and then, as the ships come together with the movement of the sea, you step from one to the other.

Again, I have no recollection of this but, come my turn, as I went to board the ship I stepped out just as the boats were moving away from each other.

By some miracle of speed and agility, the Lieutenant Commander on the scene, a guy with a big ginger beard, grabbed my arm as the ship and boat pulled apart and I was left hanging in between. He pulled me up just as the two crashed together underneath me. I then tootled off to my mess, blissfully unaware.

It's Naval tradition that, after someone's been hammered and can't remember what they've done, that you write them a list of all the things they've done and all the people they need to apologise to. It's a right piss-take and people put all sorts of things on there to wind you up.

So, I got up in the morning and looked at the list and right at the top was 'Thank Lieutenant Commander So-and-So'.

"What's this one?" I asked, looking at the Lieutenant Commander's name in my list.

58

"Saved your life."
"Fuck off!"
"Saved your life. You need to go and see him first thing."
So, I go to the officer's mess.
"Is Lieutenant Commander So-and-So in?"
He came, upright and orderly.
"Yes Utting."
"I believe thanks are in order Sir," I said, "That you saved my life."
"I did Utting, yes," he said and told me what had happened.

There have been quite a few instances in my life where it seems somebody's been watching out for me. It's just fate that I survived that accident.

If he hadn't have caught me I would have been gone, without a shadow of a doubt. If I hadn't have drowned I would have been crushed. It was a split-second action; I was walking into thin air. The only reason he caught me is that I had my hand out to get the guard rail. It was unbelievable that he managed to catch me at all.

Another of the few times I went out with the lads from the mess was in Amsterdam. Amsterdam was everything you might expect it to be. But also, a bit of a let-down. It was just too in your face for me.

It was the first time I'd seen a porn bar, the first time I'd seen live sex. I've had a couple of encounters with prostitutes – more from curiosity really, but I've not been able to get it up, I think because they didn't *actually* want me. But Amsterdam was just so overt it puts you off, which was alright if you're desperate, but I wasn't desperate, I was just doing it for the crack.

You walk in and it's almost like a factory line. Really matter of fact. She could have been sat behind a desk, for fuck's sake!

"Come in. Come in. Henry will take your money."
"Henry?! Who the fucks Henry??"
"Now just lie down and -"
"No, no, this isn't happening for me…"

There was no feeling. No compassion. There was no anything. It was obviously a highly pressurised industry. And it did nothing for me.

I also went out with the lads to a sex bar in Amsterdam. There was live action going on all around us, on the tables next to us there are people having sex, and on stage there was a girl performing with a trout. It really wasn't nice.

We sailors were all sat around the front of the stage and every time anyone on the stage ejaculated, they would flick it at you. Again, not nice. One of our group got invited up on stage but it didn't do anything for me.

There were all sorts going on, girls picking 50p coins up with their bits, shooting ping pong balls into buckets, everything you can imagine going on in Amsterdam, it was going on in that bar.

"This is Helga. This is her fish…"

"Oh, my lord!!"

It was a right spectacle, and at that age it was almost expected that you had to go. 'It's the red-light district, you've got to see the red-light district if you're in Amsterdam, that's what it's about!' that was the attitude. I imagine some people got off on it but to me, I was just thinking, 'It's not nice, this…' the whole time.

Another significant encounter I had in Holland was when i went to Den Helder. That was the first time I had Mayo on chips.

"Cone of chips, please."

"Mayo?"

"What?! No… salt and vinegar…."

"No, Mayo!"

"Oh…Whoa! Fucking hell! That's amazing!"

While in Western Europe we also spent time at the naval base in Brest in France, which was very dull. I can't remember much about being there except I know that I was there.

Later our ship was the guard ship in Gibraltar, which is a six-week duty. More alcoholics come off that duty than any other place. 'Cos it's BORING.

Gibraltar is dead. There's nothing to do. The only women there are the ones who work in the bars, Brazilians and Australians, who have been there forever, or for a long enough time that they've already fucked everyone they want to fuck. That's the impression that I got. I never even attempted to pull any. I just had an inner sense that it wasn't even worth me trying to chat them up.

Instead I just used to drink John Collins all day, big long glasses of Gin n sparkling soda – super refreshing.

The night clubs were open till 4 in the morning, but they were dead, I remember a few times sat listening to Donna Summer's *Love to Love You* with fucking nobody there.

For something to do I went to see the rock apes. They're just some monkeys. I don't know what I was expecting to see...

"Are you going up to the rock again?"

"Am I fuck! I'm going to the beach and having a drink."

So, Gibraltar... Lovely weather. Three beaches. Fuck all going on.

One of the few good things I did do in Gibraltar was go on a Banyan, which is a naval picnic. You load up one of the little punts, or sailing dinghies, with beer from the mess, and food, and you putter out somewhere, have a drink and roll it back.

I was part of the Buffer's party then, where you learned all the old skills, sail making, including sewing body bags, splicing rope and wire, all that sort of stuff. As a by-product of being in the Buffer's party you also get carte blanche first refusal on all the ship's boats because you learn to sail them.

So, four of us decided to go on a banyan to Gibraltar point, a peninsula type thing with a watchtower maybe 40 foot high. We went to the Buffer, the chief seaman.

"Buffs, can we have a ship?"

"Where're you going?"

"Going for a banyan Buffs,"

"Yeah. Alright."

The Buffer was a man of very few words. He never used one word when none would do. He could get across about 50 words with a 'Muh' and you knew exactly what he meant. He was the nearest thing to a legend I ever met. I was on one of my 'jaunts' once (AWOL) and was in an old-style sailor drinking bar in Portsmouth and the Buffs came in. He greeted me, asked if I was ok and left me to it. No judging, no histrionics.

He was about as wide as he was tall with hands as big as my head, and, myth had it, he could splice wire with his fingers. He was a massive Manchester United fan with a big black beard and a tattoo of the Red Devils on his back, not that you could see it much, for his body was covered in a mass of hair.

He always looked after his lads though and, to the seamen, he was like God. Amazing guy.

There's one story that brings home what he was to us. I was on the ship's front tying up, tying lines around bollards. You have lines, back and front, and I was on the storm hawser, the one right near the front.

At that time the Navy were changing from an old kind of rope to a different kind of rope. The old ropes used to start parting, when they were under pressure and about to break. As they were giving out, under too much strain, they gave you warning as they started parting, with a singing sound. But when they snapped they whipped back with enough force to cut your legs off, if you didn't get out of the way. The new ropes were designed to just fall apart – ping – ping – ping and then fall in bits into the water.

I was up front, on the storm hawser, with the Buffer in the middle directing operations. One of the officers, probably a midshipman, a baby officer, new to the ship and the role, shouted to me;

"That man on the storm hawser! Take a turn!"

Take a turn means take a turn and lock. You veer it, under pressure, as the ship goes forward about a quarter of a knot, with about 4,800 tons behind it, moving the rope under its own momentum. You lock it, the rope stretches, but it stops the ship from moving slightly.

Now I'd been on the storm hawser loads of times and I'm thinking 'the ships moving?! I'm not taking a turn, if it's moving away…'

"Take a turn, I said!" the officer repeated,

So, I take a turn and lock it. And the rope immediately starts going ping – ping - ping.

And I'm thinking; 'my legs are gone'.

Any minute it's going to sing, it's going to whip back and it's going to cut my legs off.

I looked up at the officer and the officer, seeing what was about to happen, put his hand up to his face and covered his eyes.

The chief seaman, the Buffer, looked at me, and then looked at the officer. And then the rope went ping – ping –ping – plop and just dropped.

The Buffer ran up the length of ship, up and out on to the bridge and grabbed the officer by the throat, dragging him out of sight. God knows what the Buffer did to him then, but we could all hear the shouting from where we were.

That officer wouldn't have known that it was a new rope. It could have killed me. He could have killed me. Baby officers are new to the job and need training. I once stood next to a baby officer during a dry dock move where he was sweating and saying to me 'First time at sea?' and I was thinking 'You pussy! It's like a millpond! We're going 500 yards; wait till you get in some heavy seas!'.

A baby officer's like anyone, they need to learn, and he made a mistake. It was an error, but probably the only person that could have stopped him was the Captain. The Buffer grabbing him was the logical reaction to me.

Buffers are like Gods on the ship, they have total authority with the working of the ship topside. Back in the day they would have been the ones that called a mutiny. Nobody stopped him when he grabbed that officer.

It was the Buffer that came back out as I was still standing on deck with my heart pounding.

"Come and have a rum in the mess." he said.

"I'm alright Buffs…"

"Come and have a rum, lad." That was pretty much an order.

"Thanks Buffs."
Always looked after his lads, the Buffer.

Back in Gibraltar, the Buffer gave the four of us a boat and we went on the Banyan.

We sailed out to this tower on Gibraltar point, like I say, easy 40 foot high. You had to climb up it and on the very top was just a flat square parapet, a piece of wood with a hole in the middle, and just enough room for you to sit in it cross legged.

The four of us sat there. And we all knew what we had to do.

Which was jump off. A forty-foot drop.

You knew that as you were climbing up. And you knew that if you didn't jump the rest were going to throw you off.

So, we were all sat there, and it was like The Good the Bad and the Ugly, all of us looking at each other, waiting to see who'd be the first to go.

The youngest guy on the ship was a young jock, obviously called Jock, he'd have been about sixteen and a bit, and he finally went;

"Fuck it, I'm going."

He jumped off and it took him about two seconds to hit the water.

One

...and

Two

Splash....

I got up, shaking but ready to go.

"R-r-right...I-I-I'll go next..."

And as I jump off, one of them shouts:

"Shark! Shark!"

Fuckers. You can imagine, it was like one of those cartoons, I was swimming in mid-air trying to climb back up as I was dropping like a stone.

I was papping myself, looking for the sharks as I'm falling, thinking I was about to die. Jaws had been out by that point, and we had all seen that, so as I was dropping I was convinced I was about to be eaten.

Obviously, there wasn't a shark and, once you'd done the jump once, you did it another four or five times. Fantastic day.

Another incident involving sharks also involved the Buffer. I made myself the ship's shark expert for 1 of our trips. When you're at sea on a big trip, everybody on board takes on a different role; entertainments officer, shark expert, whatever you take an interest in, as a leisure activity. So, I knew what a Carcharodon Carcharias was back in the day (i.e. a Great White) and I could recognize an oceanic white tip from a blue mako. So, if anyone sighted a shark they'd call me up to confirm. Two minutes after I got up there, there'd be a chef on the scene.

Anything that can be caught, a naval chef will cook. Flying fish comes over the side – fwoosh – the chef's there before it's even landed.

We were shark fishing in the Bay of Biscay, where the sea is so clear it's like a prism, you can see a shark that might be twenty foot below the surface with pin prick clarity. We'd got meat off the chef as bait and were using hand lines, which are used for passing bigger lines from ship to ship with a bolas on the end, and we've attached hooks to them to catch the sharks.

We caught two oceanic white tips, about five-foot-long each, and everyone wanted their photo taken with them. The first one we couldn't get up, so we got a cargo net halfway round it and were trying to gaff it with boat hooks.

Sharks are hard to kill, they're all muscle. The only thing that can kill it for deffo is going through its brain. The boat hooks weren't working, and the gunner wouldn't let us kill it with guns;

"You're a sailor, you're not having guns!"

So, we called the Buffer.

The Buffer was old school and always, always looked after his boys. One time, we bought him a pole cat for his birthday. It was right vicious. It bit his hand to fucking ribbons and he loved it to bits. You're not allowed animals on ship so he kept it in his equipment locker for about a month, until he eventually had to get rid of it, and no one else could even get near it apart from Buffs. Right vicious, it was.

So, if anyone could kill a shark it was the Buffer.

"What's up with you fuckers," the Buffer said as he came up.

"Buffs! We can't get this shark up!

"Giz it here!"

So, he grabbed the cargo net and dragged it up onto deck. As he got the shark on to the deck, it twisted, thrashing, and bit him on the calf. Like, really bit him. Buried its teeth in his leg.

Everybody wanted to laugh, because we're all sailors. But we all thought, as much as he liked us, if we laughed, he'd probably throw us over the side.

He never moved. He didn't even flinch. It was like a tableau frozen in time; I can see it now. He just looked, and he seemed to be looking right at me, waiting for me to laugh, I can still see his blue eyes like little tiny flints twinkling, waiting for me to go.

We were all thinking, 'Nobody say anything'.

"You alright Buffs...?"

I don't know how we managed not to laugh but we kept it in. And the Buffer took his knife out and killed the shark. That was the Buffer. Didn't even flinch. Great guy.

And of course, as soon as the shark was dead the chefs were there, knives at the ready. Like a transporter beam on the USS Enterprise, when there's food about the chefs are instantly there.

So, we had shark meat and shark fin soup. They're great chefs, Navy chefs, and they'll cook anything. You eat well on ship.

One of my other Gibraltar anecdotes involves James Coburn (not his real name but to me he looked *just* like the actor), the only person from the Navy I've ever met since leaving, and a rampant alcoholic. He had the bunk above me and the first thing I heard in the morning was the 'pssshhhhh' noise of a can opening, because he needed to have a can of beer in the morning to get himself out of bed.

He also used to handcuff himself to bars at closing time, so they'd have to serve him another drink, before he was prepared to leave. Like Whisky Walker he'd been in the Navy a long time and he'd been up and down the chain of command, due to drinking.

He looked *exactly* like James Coburn. He was probably only about 33 but looked ancient to me, which I thought was cool. Because he'd been in the Navy for so long, he knew all the places to go where old Sea Dogs go. But, like me, James always went about on his own, if for different reasons.

I pestered him for ages to take me out, everyone told me it would never happen, and that James never took anybody with him.

After a long time of pestering, he finally gave in and he took me to a bar called the Hole in the Wall in Gibraltar, which was infamous. The landlord/barman was a man called Bubbles and you can imagine what he was like...

"Darling! Darling! Come to Bubbles!!!"

And then I come trotting in with my young, clean looks.

"Oh, Jimmy! Who's this?! Who's this?!!"

"It's Steve...."

There were women draped about all over the place and I sat down, and this woman came up and started kissing me. I looked over and saw James at the bar chatting to Bubbles and then he gets up and comes over.

"Right, I'm going." He says.

"Oh...right, I'll go with you." I said, a bit confused.

"No, no," he said, "I've sold you to her," he nodded to the woman, "For three Bacardi and cokes. So, you need to stay."

"Oh, ok James," I wasn't sure about this, but I stayed, as I was told.

She took me upstairs and started doing this that and the other. Then she started getting undressed...and she had a toggle and two.

"Er....I think there's been some mistake..." I said, "No...no...I can't do this...."

She was a Ki-Tai (Kathoey) She looked attractive, but I was thinking – blimey, I've been swapping spit with a *geezer* – which as you can imagine, threw me a tad. But I wasn't up for going any further.

"No, no, no," I said, "Look, I can't touch that..."

"No. You mine. Three Bacardi and coke." She was pretty determined, "Mine. You no go. Jimmy sold you to me."

"No, no, I'm out of here!"

I ran out of the pub and down the street, looking up and down for James. I caught up with him at the next bar and it was like nothing happened.

"Alright," he looked up from his drink, "That was quick."
"You fucker!" I panted, "You fucker!"
"You wanted to come out with me...."
So that was my one and only time out with James Coburn. Pretty much nearly a legend too.

As funny as it was in retrospect, it was a lucky escape for me. One of a few, like with the boat in Jersey. Ki-Tai's in Gibraltar are well known for being very powerful, with a big society behind them that people have fallen foul of, and people have been killed for less than running out on one them who'd bought them for sex.

Like I mentioned, years later I ran into James again. I was long since out of the Navy by then and working in North Ferriby, just outside of Hull, as a bar manager in the Crest Hotel, a nice country hotel.

I was the bar manager, with a key to all the three bars, and was setting up the function room, with a wedding on, organising the whole thing, and I threw open the doors and there stood right in front of me, with his full Naval uniform on, was James Coburn.

He looked me up and down and said;
"Are they the bar keys?"
"No way!" I couldn't believe my eyes and found it hilarious that the first thing he thought of was the bar keys, "James Coburn!"
"Wow, Steve! Wow!"

I used to sleep in the hotel often, because I liked to have a drink. I had a flat in the village, but I rarely got back there. And that night was no exception.

That wedding was just a blur.

We were up all night and I kept the bar open and James never paid for a drink the whole time. He was a proper character and it was great to see him.

The Americas

My first port of call in the Americas was San Diego. A party of four of us went out (one of my few times going out in a group).

We went to a restaurant/bar during the daytime and noticed the party of Americans in front of us ordering a pitcher of beer with four glasses. We'd never seen anything like that before in Britain. A pitcher was about two and a half pints, so when it came to our turn we ordered four pitchers and four glasses.

At that restaurant was also the first time I'd ever tasted chowder, proper American chowder, which was amazing!

That night we went to a club and a guy said to me;

"You want a smoke?"

"What is it?"

"Colombian Gold." He said, "Nothing else in it. Just Colombian Gold. But it's the best you can get. It's got no side effects, no headaches, just makes you feel great."

I've had a few joints in my life since then and that was, without doubt, the best joint I've ever had in my life. I remember smoking it and grinning for the rest of the night, dancing my socks off and just having an amazing great time.

Pot was commonplace in the US.

We did exercises with the American Navy and used to do exchanges, when we were tied up next to an American ship. US ships are dry, they're not allowed alcohol. But…they all smoke pot. So, we used to swap crates for baggies, take out a buffers punt with five or six stacks of crates in return for four or five baggies. And not shit, they had the good stuff, Colombian Gold and the like.

The US ships had all the best, most up to date equipment and all the poorest trained sailors. They're fucking useless. They can't even coil rope down properly. A British sailor will coil a rope in a second, so it ends up like a Swiss roll. Americans will just chuck it on the floor.

Even to this day if I see a piece of rope that's not coiled it jives me, because if it's kinked you can't use it.

About pot, I've got a story from when I was in San Francisco.

When you arrive in a new port, you get a circular sent out to the ships company before you dock. It's called a White Paper and on it is a list of all the places where you, as a sailor, shouldn't go. So, everybody looks at the top one and obviously everybody goes there, because you're all sailors.

The top of the list was a place called the White Lights discotheque.

In the mess we had a book which was the ten best things to go to and the ten worst. According to the book this one was in the top 5 most dangerous discotheques to go to, in the World. So of course, everybody wanted to go, and we all went.

One of our crew got put down outside, because he was a knob, and some guy took him out. I left everybody when I got in there and met these two twins.

The dance floor was like a big boxing ring, with boxing ropes round the outside, and I was there dancing with these girls, and even got my photo taken with them. It was a good night.

At the end of the night they said to me;

"Daddy runs the Air Force Base. Would you like to come for dinner?"

"Fucking hell! Yeah! Course I would!"

I went to the air force base. The mother was home, but the Dad wasn't at the time. It was the first time I'd met anyone's family in the Americas and the first time I was offered iced tea. The mother offered me a glass of tea and I thought she'd just made a grammatical error and had meant to say cup. But of course, she brought me a glass of tea. I'd never tasted anything like it before. It was horrible.

"Bloody hell! Where's the milk and sugar?! It's cold!"

"Milk and sugar? Hot water?!"

"Yeah! Cup of tea!"

That was an eye opener. Back then the world was a much bigger place and an Englishman abroad was a rarity. I used to get stopped all the time and asked to talk to people just because they wanted to hear my accent. The first night out in the Americas I went to a burger bar on the way back to the ship and a girl came up to me and said, can you just come and sit and have your burger here and talk to me.

The Dad came home at lunchtime and joined us and said to me; "Steve, would you like something to drink? Smoke?"
"Smoke of what?"
And he had a baggy of cannabis. This was commonplace back then, maybe it was legal in some states, I'm not sure.
"So, you want a smoke?" he continued.
"And you run the air force base? The whole air force base?"
"Yeah, they're all my boys..." he smiled.

A little way up the coast, in Portland, Oregon, I found this club called Earthquake Ethel's. It used to open at 4 in the afternoon and played just elevator music from 4 until 8, then, at 8 o'clock, it would play the soundtrack from salsa soul, bursting into disco.

They used to have picture screens built into the walls, at the time they had the state's most expensive light and sound show, with three mirrored dance floors and on the screens, they would show pictures of the earthquake and then suddenly burst into disco.

It wasn't until I'd left the Navy, and looked it up on the internet, that I discovered it used to be a go to place for professional dancers, with pictures of people holding trophies and all sorts.

It had an age limit of 21, and I was only 17 or 18, but on my first time I went in my white front and got in. That first time I went with two other sailors and we were on the dance floor, eyeing up a group of three women. One of the sailors nudged me and asked me to go and ask them to dance.

I was quite a good dancer then. I could do a bit of shuffling, very soulful, I could do all the moves, bit of tap, all that.

So, I strolled across the dance floor and picked the tallest one.
"You dancing?"
She agreed and, as we went over to the dance floor, I asked her what she did for a living.
"Oh, I run my own dance school."

Right…..

"So," she says, "You can hustle, yeah?"
Er…No, I can't!
It was probably one of the only times I've been overpowered. I didn't know what to do. I could hear my shipmates wetting themselves while I was doing a Dad shuffle and she was flying round the floor like Flashdance. She was amazing. It was so embarrassing.

The next time I went to Earthquake Ethel's I went on my own. I saw a girl there who, the moment I saw her, I genuinely couldn't breathe. She was the archetypal bubble-gum chewing, corn-fed, All-American cheerleader. She was so attractive it was painful, not classically beautiful, but attractive; strawberry blonde hair, perfectly blue eyes, dusting of freckles across the nose. She was stunning.

As I was asking her to dance, I was already turning away. I thought, 'there ain't any fucking way she's dancing with me. No way.' But then she said;

"Sure!"

Her voice was a Texan drawl, an accent that, to me was unbelievably sexy. She had this saying that I picked up on, when she was telling me something in jest, and you were checking if she was being serious, where she'd say;

"I'm just tricking ya…" in that amazing Texas drawl. It used to melt me every time.

She took me back to hers, and she was a little bit older than me, and that first night I couldn't bring myself to have sex with her. It sounds weird but, even though I wasn't a nasty or dirty individual, or anything like that, I didn't want to sully her. I didn't want to touch her; I just wanted to look at her, even as she was asking me if I wanted to do it.

We did in the end, though. And it was amazing.

The next day she rang her Mum in Texas. In my mind I had this picture of her mum in a ranch in the middle of the desert in Texas, with woodchucks trotting around outside.

"Mom! I've met this sailor! You wanna hear his accent?"

I stayed with her in Oregon for a week and I didn't want to go back to the ship.

"I'll leave it!" I said, "I'll jump ship!"

"Steve, you can't..." she said, "You can't do that with your life. You've got to go back."

It was her that made the sensible decision in the end. She drove me back to the ship and we made love in the backseat, on the dockyard.

I must have wept for a week afterwards. I just went, completely. Totally infatuated.

We wrote for a while. She always wanted to come to England. Some of the letters tailed off, some didn't, but at some stage I'll have moved on and the letters will have stopped.

I used to be a prolific letter writer. Back then when you were at sea, getting a letter was a really big thing. Now it wouldn't have the same impact, because you'd just get a text. But back then when you'd get a letter it was a big deal. You'd get the mail brought through;

"Utting, Utting, Utting, Utting....."
"Fucking hell! Why is it always for him?!"
"....Utting, Utting...."
"Woohoo!" Winner, winner.

I used to spend hours writing letters. I'd put song lyrics in them, taken from songwriters that said something I wanted to say. I used to use a lot of Queen songs, because Freddy Mercury and Brian May were incredible lyric writers, they just used to write things that I'd think "Wow! That's what I want to say!" So, I'd use it. And women used to love it.

When I left the Navy, I destroyed everything that was associated with those times, because I wasn't there anymore, so all my letters, pictures of the ship, everything, I got rid of them all.

One of the women that used to write me letters and postcards, for a while, was a schoolteacher I'd met on the Americas trip. She was on vacation at the time, with her four friends, driving up and down the coast. She met me and one of her friends met someone else off the ship.

She used to make a big thing of my butt, telling me I had a "right cute butt".

One time she made me do it with her in her apartment, while her friend was in the next bed.

"I know she isn't asleep," she whispered to me, "I know she's not. So, we're going to do it."

I found it a real turn on that the teacher of 5th grade kids, who you'd expect to be a prim and proper school ma'am, was the complete opposite.

She started following the ship and by the second time I started getting fed up and told her to do one.

There were dangers in the Americas too. When we got to San Francisco, there was an IRA sympathizer's protest rally. These were people who had never seen Ireland in their life, rich Americans with money to burn who had Irish connections, carrying placards saying 'Release Bobby Sands' and all that sort of stuff.

It was the first time all the British warships had met up in San Francisco. They'd all gone their separate routes and met up in San Fran and now were faced with these protests.

The American police had come to the Navy and asked if they wanted to risk British sailors going ashore.

"You're not keeping these blokes locked up," was the answer.

There were rewards out for tarred and feathered officers, we were told not to accept lifts from anybody and to stay within the confines of the base.

I remember having to push past crowds with placards saying things like 'British Death Fleet Go Home'. But it was like water off a duck's back for me.

I went out and I was hitching rides and chatting to locals within five minutes of leaving the ship. And I had an amazing time in San Francisco.

There were a couple of other brushes with danger in the Americas.

At the time in the US there was a big hotel chain called Ramada Inn. I was out one time and went to the Ramada Inn, hotels were different over there, they were places you did just go to for a drink, a bit like Edinburgh, back in the day, when pubs were shut, on a Sunday for instance, because hotels could serve alcohol while the pubs were shut.

I met a woman at the hotel. She was 42, and I was still only 18, and, long story short, I gave her the 'I'm a virgin' routine. She took me home and, when we got there, she gave me a speech.
"I've got a daughter your age," she said, "Just two doors down from my bedroom. She may be younger - but she doesn't know what Mama knows..."
She was bigging herself up and promising she'd take me to heaven and back but, when it came to it, it was crap. She had a wart at the bottom of her spine, and I could feel it. It really wasn't doing anything for me.
Afterwards, I told her I wanted to go back to the ship, and she lost the plot with me then.
"You guys are all the same!" she said, "You're only after one thing!"
"It wasn't very good," I shrugged, "Did you enjoy it? It just wasn't very good..."
She drove me back to the ship and dropped me off about 100 yards short of the gangway.
"There you go," she said.
I got out and started walking and when I was about 50 yards from the car she suddenly drove at me, obviously just to frighten me. I remember running for the gangplank and then she screeched off and drove away. I probably wasn't in that much danger but that was a poor encounter.

Another near miss, and this was a real brush with danger, was when I was in Florida. I was walking down a street, not really thinking anything of it, and when I got to the far end, I saw a cop car waiting for me.
When I got to the end this cop spoke to me, asked me where I was from, what I was doing in town and then told me why he was so impressed with me being there.

"You're the first white guy who's ever walked in that street and come out." He said.

I looked back and I could see people hanging on corners and looking suspiciously out of windows. It was a drug haven. I'd had no idea. But I'd been completely safe walking through it. I can only think that, again, it must be that I don't give off that kind of vibe; I'm not seen as a threat.

While we were in Florida, based in Fort Lauderdale, I got to visit my uncle John, my Mum's brother, a white Liverpudlian, who'd gone to America and met Yolanda, a black state psychiatric nurse. They'd married and set up a state-funded private psychiatric hospital and made a lot of money from it. They lived in Dania, one of the first black and white integrated townships in the state, where your neighbour could be black. John as a white Liverpudlian with a six-foot black woman was a perfect example of that.

John came to visit me on the ship, the Buffer took him to the chief's mess and got him hammered, and he told me Yolanda wanted to take me out the next day, saying she'd come to the ship and wine me, dine me, whatever I want.

Around that time, I phoned home from Uncle John's den and I'd picked up a bit of an American accent. It's a bit corny but I tend to pick up that sort of thing, I don't know why, maybe it's the acting genes, it's not intentional but I'd just picked up that kind of drawl. I remember speaking to someone at home and just hearing;

"Talk sensible you daft bugger!"

So, the next day I got a call to the ship's gangplank;

"Able Seaman Utting! You have a visitor!"

When I get up, there's about ten of my shipmates looking down the gangplank. And what they're looking at was a cream Camaro parked at the bottom, with the door open, all cream leather interior, and leant on it, was this six-foot-tall, incredibly striking black woman.

"Tell me...tell me she's not here for you...." somebody said.

"Course she is!!" I said, "I meet her yesterday." I wasn't about to tell them she was my uncle's wife.

"Fucking hell Utting! You jammy bastard!"

I went down, and she asked me where I wanted to go.

"I don't mind Yolanda. You decide."

"Ok. Let's go shopping first. Do you like denim?"

She took me to a Levi's shop. This was the first shop I'd ever been in where you could buy a shirt that was denim, where there were pumps that were Levi's. So, she bought me everything in denim.

"Ok, what do you want to do now?" she asked, "Shall we go for dinner?"

"Yeah, yeah. I'll go for some dinner."

"Ok, I'll take you to a favourite restaurant of mine."

So, we went to a restaurant in Dania. When we got there a man in a suit came up to us and spoke to Yolanda. Yolanda was the mayoress of Dania, so she was well known.

"Yolanda, would you like a TV table? Would you like to sit somewhere near the salad bar?"

This was the first time I'd seen a salad bar, we never had them in England back then, and the first time I'd seen a TV in a restaurant.

"Would you like some salad?" Yolanda asked later.

"No, don't bother paying for that. I'll just have a meal."

"No, you don't pay for that. It's all free."

"Really? Really?! Wow!"

After five minutes chatting, the guy in the suit walked away, Yolanda leaned over to me.

"Mafia," she said, nodding in his direction, "He's a junior boss, a capo."

"Really?!"

"Yeah. This place is mafia owned." She nodded, "Never has any trouble here. You never have any trouble in Mafia bars."

"Why?"

"It's bad for business. Hurts the money. If you cause trouble here you disappear. So, it's always good."

"Wow!"

"I know the owner because I'm the mayor of Dania. So, we have a relationship."

I couldn't believe it. Mafia!

When we'd finished the meal, Yolanda asked where I wanted to go next.

"I want to go in a record shop!"

Quite a lot of record shops over there were under their own labels, so Universal would have a Universal record shop and in there would be a million records, all under that label. RCA would have a record shop that was all RCA.

We went in this record shop. Rows and rows, about 30,000 square feet, of vinyl.

"Pick what you want," Yolanda said.

I used to like soul at the time and so I used to like buying stuff I'd never heard of. I was looking through these records and saw this one LP and what caught my eye was that the band on the front were all dressed as Red Indians, colourful. The band were called Sweet Thunder, I don't remember the album name, so I picked that.

So that was my day with Yolanda.

A day or two later we had these cops come to the ship, to walk round it. I struck up a friendship with this black cop called Melvin;

"Can I hold your gun?"

"No, you can't."

"Can I go on your motorbike?"

"No. But I will walk you round the precinct. You can meet all the guys."

"Oh yeah! Brilliant!"

He came back to the ship and took me to the precinct to meet the guys, as promised. Afterwards, he offered to take me back to his apartment where his wife would cook us some tea and then go out to a club afterwards.

At his apartment he showed me his police manual, which was about the size of three telephone directories with a full chapter on how to speed load your gun. It was all amazing to me. After tea he said to his wife that he was taking me to Big Daddy's. She seemed a bit bemused by that, but I didn't know why.

We drove down and stopped at a traffic light on the way. As we did, some black guys leaned over the car.

"Yo blood! How's it hanging?" they all knew Melvin and they all knew he was a cop. He carried a pearl handled revolver, which was illegal, but he seemed to get on with everybody.

"Who's the white dude?" they asked.

"He's a brother from the ship," Melvin said, "He's cool. He's from England."

"Wow, dude!" they seemed genuinely welcoming.

What I found was that black and gay guys over there didn't have a chip on their shoulder. If you wanted to know where the best disco was you asked a gay guy and the black guys were all comfortable with whom they were.

So, we got to Big Daddy's and it was a club cut into a wall, you'd go down a kind of cavern and about halfway down was a little hole with a guy sat behind it.

Melvin says to me;

"Go down there; ask for a ticket," my Uncle works behind the counter, "Just tell him you want a ticket. Just play it out. Tell him you want to come in."

So, I went down and, when he saw me, the guy behind the counter's eyes almost dropped out of his head. He couldn't speak for about ten seconds.

"You can't go in there!" he said.

"Yeah yeah, I want a ticket!" I said, no idea what was up.

"No, no, man..." he shook his head, "You can' go in there dude..."

Then Melvin came up behind me.

"It's alright, he's with me," he said.

The guy behind the counter saw the funny side then. What I didn't know was that it was an all-black club.

As Melvin took me in he told me I could dance with whoever I wanted, everybody's cool, but don't pull. Don't try to do anything. Just be cool.

In the middle of the dance floor was a pyramid with lights on that slowly revolved. About halfway through the night the DJ called out;

"Come and get your bottle of champagne Steve. Let's have a hand for the only white guy in the place!"

I stood up and I was the only white guy there.

"He's a brother from the ship, here with my cousin Melvin. Show him a good time."

The club also had live bands and, while we were sat there, these druids came out, or they looked to me like druids, with cowls over their faces. And just as the DJ was saying "Put your hands together for...." they threw their cowls off and they were all in Red Indian gear.

"...Sweet Thunder!"

I turned to Melvin and said;

"You're not going to believe this, but I know these! I bought their record yesterday!"

Out of all the million records in the store I'd picked that one and there they were on stage. Amazing.

Further down the coast we visited Mexico. This was the first time I'd been offered cocaine in a McDonalds. It was rife. It was like every film you've ever seen in a third world country where drugs were everywhere.

"There's a policeman over here!" I'd said. But the guy just shrugged.

"He's on the take," he said. They all were.

I mentioned earlier that of the three times I'd been with prostitutes, I couldn't do it, two out of those three times.

I was once with some friends in a pub talking about what was the fastest we'd ever got anyone into bed and what our best chat up lines were.

Everybody was saying things like 'a day' or whatever. I went '10 seconds'.

"How did you manage that? What was that chat up line?"

"*How much?*'"

Now in Amsterdam I hadn't been able to do it, it was too blatant and professional. In the Americas I had my other two experiences of prostitution. The one in the US was one of those few occasions I'd gone out with someone else. We'd walked into a massage parlour, without really thinking what that meant, and asked for a massage.

"Are you armed?" the woman on the door asked.
"Am I what?"
"Have you got a gun?" she said, "You can't take guns in there."
"Have I fuck got a gun! I'm English!"
It turned out it was a mafia run brothel. The woman talked me through the process and I quickly realised what sort of place I was in.

I went in to see the prostitute and made the mistake of being sympathetic.
"Why do you feel you have to do this?" I'd said, I must have seemed really gauche, "You're really nice…"
"I've got a child at home and I've got no other talent…"
That was it then, I couldn't have got it up for love or money. She tried but I told her not to bother, that we'd just lie there for a bit and talk.

The Mexican I met in Nassau was different. I'd been chatting her up at the bar beforehand and really fancied her. She was hot. Really hot. The fact she was a prostitute was probably secondary to the fact that I wanted her.
"It'll cost you," she'd said.
"Fucking hell! Yeah!"
And it was amazing. Tight and oily. Winner, winner.

The Tropics

There was a myth going around that year, before we set out, that a ship beginning with 'B' would go down.
During the Americas trip we went across the Bay of Biscay.

The Bay of Biscay I always remember as somewhere you could top up your tan. Obviously, you had to be careful, because getting sunburn on board ship was a risky business, as it would be classed as a self-inflicted injury, and you'd have your pay docked as punishment for that.

I used to go up to the top deck and you'd have just ten minutes either side, front and back, before you were in danger of burning. The sun would be directly above you, in the middle of the sky, at the top, something i had never seen before, since it was my first time in that locale.

I thought it was incredible. I always liked the fact that everywhere you looked, if it was a quiet, calm day, you couldn't see anything. You couldn't see a horizon, the water was pale blue, the sky was pale blue, and you were just looking out into infinity. It was like being in a bubble, but a bubble without any edges.

Partly because of that peace and silence, I used to like doing lifebuoy ghost duties. The lifebuoy ghost is a lookout, during the night watches, posted on the quarter deck, just below the flight deck. You're connected to the bridge via radio and all you're looking out for is a splash. If you see or hear a splash, you tell the bridge and you throw over a lifebuoy and that's why you're called a lifebuoy ghost. Obviously in the Arctic there was no need of a lifebuoy ghost because, as I mentioned, if you go overboard, you're gone.

When I was on lifebuoy ghost duties, I would take music with me. It was back in the '70s when Saturday Night Fever was out, and I had the soundtrack. I'd stand at the edge of the ship watching the propeller wave, which would come up 20, 30, 40 feet, depending on the ship's speed, and I couldn't hear anything else, apart from the music, if the music was on, or, if I turned it off, you could just hear the whoov-whoov-whoov of the prop and the waves being churned. Just really calming.

I could imagine I was on my own, just floating above the sea. I used to love the peace and tranquillity it gave me.

With my health anxiety now, I don't go anywhere that's a danger, so going back to that is unimaginable. But back then I used to love being 'alone' at sea.

When you're abroad and you stop somewhere, before you go into port, you anchor up and clean the ship. The navy's all about looking good; 'a clean ship's a fighting ship' and all that, so before you dock anywhere you make the ship presentable. And you'd be amazed how dirty a ship's side gets.

So you stop out at sea and then go over the side in a bosun's chair, which is simply a bit of wood on the end of a rope, like you used to hang from a tree as kids and you'd use long-toms or short-toms, and you paint the ship.

When we were stopped in the Tropics, the water was so clear you could also clearly see any sharks, although refracted so you couldn't tell how far down, they were. I particularly remember seeing hammerhead sharks. Incredible.

Sometimes you get permission to bathe, which means you can jump off the side of the ship and swim round. Because it's in perilous waters, you have motorboats with gunners on, and spotters, looking for sharks. You'd think that would stop you from swimming, but it never did.

Obviously, no one shouts sharks unless there is one, because it's not that sort of environment.

But we were still sailors…

What we would do is lower someone in the bosun's chair, and below them they would be able to see sharks in the water, and then we kept lowering them. Because of the refraction of the water you can clearly see sharks, but you can't see how far away they are, because they look so small. So, you'd keep lowering and keep lowering, closer and closer to the water, and, of course, the bloke being lowered would have tears in his eyes and be shouting up to you;

"There's a shark!"
And you'd be shouting back;
"It'll be alright! Have a dip of your toes!"
I've seen grown men, well, more like grown boys, in tears asking to be let back up.
We'd insist that everybody had to have a go.
"Just send me down and pull me up quick. Get on with it…"

There was also a tradition to be taken into the aft steering compartment, the tiller flats. This was where the ship could be steered, by radio, directed from above, if the bridge got hit.

In there is an inspection plate, about 6 or 8 foot long. Under that inspection plate is an 8-inch thick plexi-glass bubble. Under that is the propeller. They use this to inspect the yaw, pitch and attitude of the propeller for sea trials.

Because the RPs' nest is above it, for special people only, they put you in it, when you're at sea. That remains probably one of the most frightening things that have ever, ever happened to me.

It was in the tropics, with clear skies and clear seas, and it feels like you're in the water. Even now, when I see disaster films on the telly, of ships at sea, and you see the size of things that shouldn't really be in the water, there's something terrifying about it.

When you're like that, flat on your front, and you can see the tip of the propeller, it's like you're going to fall on it. You've just got to stand the fear.

The noise in there was incredible. A single propeller, with blades about 30 feet high. You could always tell, anywhere in the ship, when they were putting extra PCLs on the engine. Two Rolls Royce gas Olympic Turbines, you know about it when they've upped the ante. You could feel it in your core.

You come out all bravado, going 'Go on, put me back in, you fuckers!'
'Oh alright, in you go….'
'No! No! Only joking…!'
I can feel my heart racing just thinking about it again.

With that engine and propeller, the ship had a maximum speed of over 30 knots. That's about 35 miles an hour. For a ship that is fast. Really fast. If you're stood on the back of the ship, looking out from the flight deck, the wake of the ship comes up to an incredible height.

I've steered the ship hard during sea trials, it's like a speed boat. It doesn't feel real.

When you steer a ship, you're steering to the lubber's line. You steer to a point and that point is determined by the lubber's line, a moving point on a compass. You'll steer up to a point, determined by the lubber's line, but as you turn right the lubber's line goes left. I know that if I turn right for ten seconds and go back and it'll drift back. It's quite difficult to do but you get a feel for it. It's also amazing how small the 'wheel' is for the ship – it's just like an aircraft wheel – tiny.

Any seaman doing an eight-hour stint might be called on to steer the ship as part of their duties. There's a skill to it so the skipper's always glad to see someone who's done it before.

Near the Bay of Biscay, while we were still in that stretch of clear blue ocean, we had an encounter with a Harrier Jump Jet. I believe it was on exercise from another ship in our group.

We were all called to the top deck and told that the Harrier was coming to see us. They were new then and we'd never seen anything like it.

You've got no reference point, as there's only sea and sky, which was an azure blue, so there's no reference point of size. And, off the port amidships, was an aircraft, in greens and browns that looked like God had just picked it up and popped it in the sky. A Harrier.

He was hovering in a forward motion, in line with the ship, matching speeds. It was like he was glued in space.

Everything was that bright, it was like having Ultra HD TV after an old '50s TV set and we could see him looking over. It reminds me now of Top Gun. Coolio.

There was no point of reference for it, although he was obviously close. It was pin-prick clear, like a jewel in the sky. You couldn't take your eyes off it.

And then he tipped us a salute and it just went up and away and out of sight. Everybody wanted to be a pilot after that.

Type 42's, like the Birmingham, carried a Lynx helicopter. The ship's helicopter pilot was a steely-eyed handsome devil of a junior officer called Lieutenant Rick Bull.

He used to buzz the ship's bridge, which you shouldn't do, but the skipper used to let him get away with it, because he was a real cool dude.

He also used to go on runs ashore and sometimes you'd meet him in a bar, and he'd have a drink with you, which for an officer was rare.

But there was another reason we thought he was cool. The myth was that we carried a 500-pound nuclear depth bomb as a deterrent against nuclear submarines and, if the helicopter pilot had to drop the depth bomb, he was expendable.

The mathematics were, since he had to drop it below a certain height, to get it into the sea to deliver it to the submarine, it meant that he couldn't get out of the blast area before it went off.

And he knew that. We all thought that was cool, that he knew he was expendable.

"Wow! Rick! What happens if you have to…you, know…? Wow!"

Barbados was a tale of two halves. We went to the Barbados Hilton, until we were thrown out, and, while we were there, Isaac Hayes, the guy who wrote the theme from Shaft, was staying in the same hotel.

But, at the same time, there were the slums. I remember seeing about 30 or 40 black youths, all wearing the same sort of t-shirt, with no shoes on their feet, hanging around on the street corner, because they had nowhere else to go and nothing to do and not a penny between them. I'd never seen anything like that before then.

The visit to the Hilton was short-lived. There were guys working their way round the bars playing guitars and we told them to do one, just the once. One of them wasn't having any of it and so one of us took his guitar and lobbed it over a nearby balcony – and we were asked to leave. So, we made our way down to the beach.

The beaches were gorgeous. It was the first time I'd ever seen white sand. And the beach bars were brilliant. They were literally just a bit of a hut with a rattan or leaf roof and the beer or spirits kept in holes in the sand to keep cool.

Just as dusk was coming, little tiny white crabs used to come out of holes, all the way along the beach. You could see them, thousands of them, like soldiers, marching across the beach. Stunning place.

When we got to Acapulco, there was a cruise liner there called the USS Princess and there were people there who had paid $3000 dollars for a Caribbean cruise and I was being paid to be there, I always remember having that conversation with some tourists and thinking how lucky I was.

On the way back to one of the ships in the area one of the sailors had jumped off the boat, which was ferrying sailors from ship to shore, to show off and tried to swim to the ship. He never made it.

Two days later we got the call that this guy had been seen just out from the harbour, out at sea. The buffers party were told to get one of the divers kitted up, take a boat and recover him. His own ship didn't want to do it because he was a shipmate. I believe their skipper made the call, as he deemed it too upsetting for his buddies.

If you have ever seen a body in the water after three days in the sun and heat, it's not nice. From a distance, it looked like a tailor's dummy bobbing in the swell, stiff and unmoving.

It was bloated up and criss-crossed with burnt skin, his mouth was wide open, and you could see blood up to the lip line. I always remember he had a crucifix on that was stuck in his neck.

Note – I thought long and hard about including this but felt it shaped my future health anxiety and fear of death.

I never got involved in bringing him up, but I was there in case I was needed. Bones Malone, one of the ship's divers, went down and put him in a cargo net and the Buffer pulled him up.

His parents were advised that he would be best buried at sea and that we would do that on the Birmingham.

In order to be buried, they're put in a sail, a shroud with a weight sewn in, which is traditionally what sail makers did in the Navy and sent off into the water. They had to break his arms and legs to put him in it.

At the burial I was there on the deck, in my best dress, with the music playing and then off he goes, over the side, just like in the movies. He wasn't known to us, but he was part of our naval family and it was quite sombre on ship for a while. RIP.

I remember the ship smelling of formaldehyde for weeks afterwards. At that age, of course, you think you're immortal, that it'll never happen to you. But you're never that far from danger.

I used to lead a charmed life and in hindsight, Nassau was no different.

When we got to Nassau we were told not to go anywhere outside of the half a mile area around the dockyard. As is my want, I got ashore on this bright and colourful Caribbean island and got in the first taxi I found and asked to be taken to the best club on the island.

"No, no, you can't go there," the driver shook his head, "Very dangerous. AND you're white."

"No, no, I want to go," I insisted.

"Other side of the island," he said darkly, "You might not come back."

"Yeah, yeah, I want to go there!" I didn't even think of the danger. So, he took me.

When I got there, I hit the dance floor straight away and after a while, noticed this mahoosive black dude watching me intently.

Later I was sat at a table and he came over. He was huge, around 6'4", and when he spoke, he had a lisp.

"I've been watching you danthe," he lisped, "Very nithe. Very nithe. Would you like a drink?"

"Yeah, I'll have a Tom Collins," I said, "Big 'un. Loads of ice."

"Tho you're thailor from the thip?" he asked.

"Yeah, yeah!"

"I take you home?" he said, "Take you home with me? Make you feel good?"

"Oh, no, no, thanks," I was as diplomatic as I could be.

"Yeth, yeth, yeth!" he insisted, "You don't have to do anything! I make you feel good. You know what I'm thaying? Make you feel good....?"

"Let me just tell you right now," I answered, "I'm only interested in women. You seem a nice guy, but it just doesn't do it for me. Not in any way, shape or form. Just no."

He accepted I wasn't going to change my mind and then gave me the same advice that Melvin had given me in Florida.

"Danthe with anybody," he said, "But don't do anything. Because they kill you. They'd kill you here."

Riiiight.

But I had a great night. At the end he came over again.

"I take you back to the thip?"

Now I think about this, years later, I realise the danger. He seriously must have been 6'4"/6'5", he towered over me. I didn't know the island. He could have taken me anywhere. He could have raped me, killed me, anything.

He took me right to the bottom of the ship's gangplank.

As he dropped me off he just told me how much he'd enjoyed meeting me and to tell all my friends and I was just left thinking 'Wow! What a nice guy!'

Anything could have happened that night but instead I just had a great time. Someone was deffo looking over me.

Able Seaman: Radar

As I said earlier, for my first ship I had to put aside my eight weeks of china graph radar training and learn the new ADAWS computer system. ADAWS was the first generation of an automated data weapons system.

For some reason I really connected with computer training. This was in the days before computers were everywhere. You'd be amazed by a ship's computer layouts in the '70s. It was like Close Encounters of the Third Kind, new stuff that you'd never seen before. It looked futuristic, because it was.

The layouts on the ships, the plots we'd been china graphing, were plots on screens, and we had tracker balls instead of mice, with a keyboard. You'd then inject stuff into the keyboard to process information on the screen. It was like Star Wars but back then, when you never saw anything like that in the real world.

I was good at memorising injection code.

If you're at sea and you're on exercise, or in war time, anything like that and you're on the sea plot, your Commander could say to you.

"Seaman, I'd like a guard ring put around the ship at five miles."

That means that you've put something into that computer so that if anything comes through that guard ring it'll automatically tell you. You don't have to track it on radar; you'll just know it's come through the guard ring.

To put that guard ring in place is a piece of code that was about half a paragraph (this was back in the day; it was probably ASCII or something like that).

But I would be 'tap-tap-tap' "Done sir!" in a matter of seconds. I was fucking red hot.

The radar guy is the only one who can sit in the Captain's chair. That's because, when the Captain goes to the bridge, his plot has everything on it that the radar guy, the sonar guy and the gunner guys see on their plots. The radar guy is the only guys in the ops room that must learn pieces of everyone else's role. So, I have to learn how to read a sonar plot, I have to learn how to read a gunnery plot and I have to learn how to read sea maps for the navigator's plots. RP's are the only ones in the Ops Room that have to do that; you don't know that until you join the ship.

If the Skipper fucks off to the bridge, the Ops Room supervisor, the radar guy, who's on his own plot with two guys next to him, goes on the Captain's chair, which is a big fuck off chair, like you'd expect, and you have the plot. And I used to love that, on the odd occasion I was asked to do it.

When we were navigating the English Channel, and the English Channel's one of the busiest shipping lanes in the world, I would plot the ship through the English Channel, with two plots. And I would do it through this injection process of tagging the radar blips, continuously.

I knew that the guy next to me would be PC pos-injecting about every 10 to 15 seconds; I would do it continually, and well, because I liked it. So, I would PC Pos-inject all the time.

You're on a closed Nesta circuit to the bridge, so the skipper or First Officer would say to me;

"What's the closest point of approach with the British Respect – the tanker?"

And I would have it immediately. I wouldn't have to go, and PC pos-inject, I just had it. Because my whole plot was live and up to date. That took incredible concentration. But I was in that zone all the time I was in there. Therefore, it was such a quandary for my officers when I was up at Captain's table.

I was good at sea, I really was. The only issue was, once the ship got to port, I was off.

I never made it to Leading Hand, I could have done it, and people wanted me to do it, but I didn't put the time in to take the test.

On that Ops Room role, during the Falklands, when the HMS Sheffield and Coventry were hit, there were civvies moaning, asking why they couldn't detect the missiles, given that they had long range radar, short range radar and even lookouts.

We used to do exercises at sea against aircraft that fire dummy missiles and detecting those was incredibly hard. Having done exercises with dummy missiles I know that the people in that Ops Room may not have seen it or seen it too late. The radar return on a missile, especially on land or above waves is like a millimetre. It's intermittent, here and gone. You're lucky if you get three sweeps of it. On top of that, an Exocet goes up and then dips down, below the radar. Once it's down, you're buggered.

We also used to do exercises where we'd do submarine spotting. You'd win a crate of beer if you spotted a periscope when it came up. And there weren't many crates of beer being handed out. You'd get maybe two sweeps of it, you'd know it was something different, because you're used to what the radar looks like. And then it's gone.

That's how hard it is. The crew of that Operations Room on the Coventry would have had a slim chance of detecting the missile that hit them. And that's where I would have been during the Falklands, if I'd have still been in the Navy. The Coventry was due to have been my next ship. RIP.

That's another time where I've been lucky. People died in there and one of them would most likely have been me. Just like that street in San Francisco that I walked down safely or trusting myself in the hands of the massive gay guy in Nassau or running out on that kitai in Gibraltar without coming to any harm, lots of little instances where I feel like I've led a charmed life. Or just been lucky.

Later, because of my skill with the computer radar systems, I got a posting to HMS Osprey, the naval air base, the base for the Blue Berets, or powder puffs as we called them, the airmen for the Naval arm, and it was my favourite time in all the Navy.

It was based in Weymouth, on Portland Point, and I did about nine months there, which included the summer. I had a room in a house in the village, which I paid for, where I could sleep, rather than staying on site and my days were something like 9 until 2 and then the rest of the time was my own.

My job was helicopter controller trainer. On each ship that has a helicopter you have a helicopter controller. This is the guy who sits in front of a radar screen linked to the helicopter. If anything goes wrong with the helicopter you have certain commands that are passed down, he gives instruction to the helicopter and it's like an umbilical cord between the controller and the pilot.

As with most things, the British Navy training for this was the best in the world, so we used to get European Navies sending helicopter controller potentials to the base.

You'd have two or three portacabins, all rigged up with different computers in, one pretending to be the ship, one was the helicopter. They'd be the helicopter and we'd throw issues at them. We used to train them and then we'd score them.

At the time I didn't know why I got the job, I just thought 'what a brilliant posting' but it was probably because, as I've said, I was good on the computer, so I really took to it.

We used to get the Dutch Navy, German Navy, all sorts, and we'd delight in giving them the most difficult scenarios.

Of course, one of the worst scenarios is total loss of communication with the aircraft. So, we'd just turn everything off and then wait. They had certain patterns to fly in the sky to tell you what was wrong, so you waited for them to do it and when they did it you then threw something else at them

"What shall I give 'em now?"

"Give 'em rotor trouble and an oil leak..."

As part of that job you got to go up in a Wessex helicopter and, even though I was fearless then, it's still a very intense experience. There's a song by Harvey Danger called My Private Helicopter, which has the line "Pretty little bubble in the sky". And that's what it is, a bubble. You're thinking 'Bloody hell, there's about 4 mil of aluminium between me and nothing, up here'.

I got to have a go on the stick and, now that I'm a drummer, I can understand more the difficulties of flying a helicopter, because you've got yaw and pitch, which are opposite directions, which you control with your feet and the yoke which you control with your hands... All I got was the control yoke and told to hold it steady. But as soon as you get control of it you can feel it trying to get away from you, you just go into a panic and you can't help thinking; 'Wow! Helicopter pilots are right dudes.

One of my other more interesting postings was guarding the War House. This was a big house somewhere in the South, in a country estate, surrounded by a moat, where the Prime Minister would go to dictate operations in the event of war.

It was part of a big land exercise and my brief was to be on an outpost, in a delve in the ground under a blanket, watching for anybody coming around. We were told the SAS were going to come in and storm the house as part of their training. Of course, we'd all heard the myths about them;

"Don't let them find you Steve. They'll stick a flash bang up your arse and fucking put you in a hole in the ground."

"They don't mess about these boys. Don't let them find you…"

I had my headset on, lying flat in a hole in the ground and then I saw them. They'd passed me and got over the moat to get to that point. You know, I never heard them. But there they were. Four of them.

It was one of those moments where you just think;

"Wow…! …. Don't say a fucking word…. Don't speak. Don't say anything. They're the boys. They're the SAS boys."

What I wanted to say was:

"Guys! Guys! Hang on a minute! You never saw me, did you?"

But obviously I didn't. Nobody wants a flash bang up their arse.

But I still haven't mentioned some of the best parts of my posting in Weymouth. My time there was fantastic partly because of my naval work, but mostly because of my life after I clocked off.

It was mostly in the summer and I used to get the bus straight down to Weymouth city centre. The house was on the Esplanade, a shared place, but the time I used to spend there was negligible, as you can imagine.

I used to go in a lot of bars in Weymouth and the one that stands out was the Victoria Bars (which is where I met D, my later fiancée). There was a downstairs, which was like a hotel bar, and upstairs, which was like a disco bar.

I met the landlord, who was an ex-marine, called Mo. He was a proper medallion man. He used to sleep around, and his wife was a gorgeous stunner who was an obvious doormat. She was a lovely, lovely lady who used to worship the ground he walked on. Even in my state I used to look at Mo and think 'you twat'. He used to get away with murder and she used to love him for it. They remind me now of Dirty Den and Angie from East Enders.

To be fair, he was a handsome guy. Very magnetic. But still.

Mo taught me some dirty fighting, close-up stuff that he learned in the marines. I ended up getting a job with him, all quite legal in the Navy; you just declare it and they tax you on it. He wanted me to be the doorman of the disco bar. It involved vetting people on the way in and taking their dosh.

The DJ was a half caste guy called Kevin, a smooth operator. We developed a real bond;

"I'll give you a shout Steve if I want them girls to come in free," he would say, "You give me a shout if you want anyone in free. Charge all the guys, all the time, full price."

I was known as the dancing doorman. I used to stand at the door and take people's money while I used to boogie. They'd put my favourite record on, Don't Stop 'Til You Get Enough, and I'd dance. I had a whole routine for it. Even Kevin, who was a good dancer, liked me to do it. I'd go in clubs in Weymouth and people would come up to me and ask me to do it. I was a proper good dancer.

There was a bar girl who worked downstairs at the Victoria Bars, called Karen, who would only sleep with black guys because only black guys would do it for her.

Also, in the Victoria Bars, I'd met this girl called Tina who lived around the corner on the esplanade, in a house full of students, and I found myself sleeping with those students.

It was like Bruce Lee's Game of Death, where he fights his way up a house, floor by floor. My Game of Death was sleeping with everyone in the house, working my way up. And on the top floor was Tina, who owned it, and she was the last one I slept with.

Back then I never had any issues with jealousy, because it was never like that. I was always really open with everybody, I was always personable, I never promised anybody anything, whenever I told anybody I felt a lot about them I really meant it, and then the next day I might feel that way about somebody else.

Whilst in one of my therapy sessions much later, I brought up the fact I felt guilty about the way I slept around. The therapist, a woman, asked if anyone had been hurt – or did we all have a good time? 'There's your answer, Steve'.

Anyway, I walked into the Vic Bars one afternoon and there was Karen behind the bar, slim, dark hair, proper looker, proper horny looker. You'd think 'fucking hell, I bet that goes like a train', she just had that aura about her. But she'd only sleep with black guys.
'Hi Karen, pint of bitter please.'
She started looking at me significantly from behind the bar.
"What's up?"
"Tina…" she started.
"Oh yeah?"
"She says you fuck like a rabbit."
"Oh…" I didn't know what else to say, and I blushed, which is always a winner.
"Yeah," she kept the significant look going, "Like a rabbit she says."
"Oh, that's very nice of her…"
I don't remember exactly what I said. But I knew what she meant. The implication was there. We could do it if I wanted.
I made the mistake of telling Mo.
"No way," he said, "She only sleeps with black dudes. She won't even sleep with Kevin and he's half-caste."
"I'm telling you. It's on. Can I borrow your flat?" I asked.
"When?"
"Tuesday night."
He thought about it for a moment.
"Yeah. Alright then." he said, "For the guys."
That was what it was like. Do it for the guys.

Tuesday night, he'd left a bottle that looked like Sangria, on the side. To this day I don't know if he did it on purpose or not, but it was a mix. I was quite nervous, so I'd knocked back quite a bit of it. It wasn't just Sangria; it was a proper mix.

The last thing I remember was lying in the bed and then she literally jumped on top of me and... that was it. I was unconscious.
I woke up in the morning thinking 'fucking hell! Fuck it!'
Karen wasn't best pleased with me either.
"You pussy!" she yelled.
And that was my chance gone.
Afterwards I confronted Mo.
"What did you put in that bottle, you git?"
"Bit of Dutch Courage," he said.
"You bastard. It knocked me out! I never did it! I never did it!"
That incident aside, that posting really was one of the highlights of the Navy for me. But there were down sides to all the hedonism too. Things I've not yet mentioned.

Fighting Man

As I've mentioned, I went all in with kung fu and karate when I was about 14. When I was in the Navy this came in useful again.
During basic training at HMS Dryad I did a boxing trial.
Fighting's always frightened me. It's a strange thing, I don't like being hit, I didn't like being in the environment, but I like the form, the kata, I like being able to fight but not doing it.
If I had to do it, I could do it.
But boxing was different.
It was a big room and they just chucked some gloves on you.
"Right, you two – Get going!" it was as organised as that.
They put me in with this guy and I took on a karate stance. And then he hit me in the throat, by accident. The moment that happened I saw red mist. So, I karate punched him, back fist, and then roundhouse kicked him in the ribs, and he went down like a sack of potatoes.
"Brilliant!" the trainer shouted, "Brilliant! Controlled aggression! Like it! Like it! You're in!"
"I'm not sure I want to do this…" I mumbled, "He hit me in the throat…"
"Yes, yes, yes, he hit you in the throat…" the trainer carried on, "Don't worry, we'll have you…"
The guy I went with, a guy called Tug, was one of those fighters who goes in with his fists raised high. He was brought up on a farm and taught bare knuckle boxing by his Dad, who was a traveller.
He came out with his fists up and everyone was laughing at him, and I thought he looked cool. And then he knocked his opponent out cold.
"Get in Tug!"
"Right, you two!" the trainer said, pulling me and Tug to one side for future training.

There's loads of training between each bout to get you up to the level needed. I had a hard punch for my weight, but I couldn't move round the ring. My trainer put a stick between my legs, tied my shoelaces together, he did everything he could. He brought in the Olympic Naval coach, Topsy Turner, and told him that I had all the qualities needed to be a boxer except I couldn't move round the ring.

To move round the ring your feet need to be equidistant, because you may need to come of the back foot to throw a punch and it's difficult to fire punches off if you're not in the right position. In karate, punches are all in the hip, boxing is slightly different. But you've got to be able to move out of the way in boxing and if you can't move out the way you'll get tagged.

So, I'd had lots of instances where the trainer had just given up and said 'I can't do fuck all with him... Let him get hit, bring 'em on and knock 'em out.'

And that's what I used to do. Of course, getting hit hurt and when I got hurt I'd get annoyed.

My game plan in all the six fights I ever fought was get in there and unload my big bombs. I started out by punching downstairs, and then wait for their guard to drop and get in there.

First, I'd body shot – hard (I used to practise with middle weights) – and then their arms would come down, it was just automatic, and then I'd be on them like snot and the referee would have to pull me off.

So, the few fights I had, and I think I only lost one, were the same premise.

I've only got little hands, I got called 'cat's paws', but the power generated through that level of aggression just caught everyone off guard.

The Olympic trainer Topsy Turner, said that for my height and weight, I had one of the hardest right hands he'd ever felt. I knocked the pads off the trainer's hands when sparring, it was controlled aggression but very high aggression, and he literally had to stop me.

At the end of the training sessions you got paired with a seasoned boxer. I'd been there about a month and they decided I was ready to be paired with a boxer called Tap Tap.

Before we got paired, the trainer came over and said, "No, you'll hurt Tap Tap".

And at that point I knew I could do this, or that I could make a stab at it.

I didn't want to get in the ring for the sake of it. I did it because I was told I was good at it. I did it also because when you're a boxer in the Navy you get a blue card, which meant I didn't do many duties (just toy work in the Petty Officer's mess) you get the best food and, because you get the best food and training, you feel amazing.

I used to clean the Petty Officers mess as duty, including the snooker tables. So, I'd give it a quick clean in the morning and then play snooker until my next training session. As for the food, you went to the front of the queue for all your food and get protein high food, like chicken. Naval food is good anyway but as a boxer I got the best of that.

The way I fought was I just wanted it over with as quickly as possible. Take as few punches as I could and then trust in my aggressive ability and fast hands. Really, what I wanted to do was dance around the ring and have a bit of a tap, because that's ok, that's safe. But when the violence starts, the blows start coming, whenever I've been put in that situation, I've beaten my fear.

But other boxers saw it differently. One time I had encounter with someone on the camp and I didn't know who he was, but he knew who I was

"I'm going to fucking do you!" he came at me pointing and yelling.

"Who the fuck are you?"

"I'm fighting you next week!" he shouted.

"Alright dude!" I couldn't understand his aggression, "Steady on! What's up with you?"

That way of thinking was alien to me. Although, of course, I did him a week later. Winner, winner.

So, I don't like being hit and I don't like that conflict. I like the feeling of confidence boxing or martial arts gives you, and the sense that you can execute something very effectively. But I didn't want to fight anybody.

That dislike of fighting I can only attribute to my childhood. It was a really big thing in my childhood years that I would protect the name of my father. At school, everyone knew not to call me a bastard, because I took it as a family slur. I guess it was a defensive reaction to the news about my parents, I don't really know.

I always remember watching Billy Connolly on Parkinson. It was a seminal moment for me.

"There's something you want to say Billy, isn't there?" Michael Parkinson said, "About your father?"

"Yeah...I was abused as a child," Billy said.

You could hear the intake of breath from the audience.

"I didn't know I was abused," he said, "because it wasn't physical as much as mental. And I didn't know until I married Pamela and she told me, and I realised, and it devastated me."

I turned to my wife Trisha and said;

"That's me! That's me!"

I can still remember the feeling in that moment. I guess I had something to hang my issues on.

Dad was a massive part of my life because he was so overbearing. So, for some reason, in the same way that I said to a psychologist, "Don't say owt about my Dad," I would say to people 'you call me a bastard again and I'll fucking drop you'. And I've done it to folk, too.

I was once in a pub with a guy who I reckon would have wiped the floor with me, a big nasty fucker, and he's said something about my Dad and the fella I was with just said 'Fucking hell!' and walked away, knowing how I'd react. I was about twenty-three or four at the time.

Part of me was frightened, part of me wanted to do him, and part of me was thinking 'Yeah, you know, you're fucking right'.

He was dissing my Dad, because he was frightened of him because my Dad had done him a while before, which I learned later.

"He's just a big bully, your Dad," this guy was saying.

The guy I was with was trying to calm me down while a big part of me was thinking 'Yeah, he's frightened you as well, hasn't he?'

As I say, I never liked conflict. I don't like it now.

As part of being in retail management, which I've done as long as I can remember, I deal with conflict, as part of managerial responsibility. But I deal with it as a process.

As a manager you have a certain amount of referent authority, so that's what I use to deal with conflict.

If I have conflict now, which I occasionally will with my gaffer, I can't give him my side of the story without being blunt. There's no gentle in slope to that, I've stood it for 50 times and then I've gone. It takes people by surprise, the force of it seeming to come from nowhere. But I'll have stood annoyance for any number of times without saying anything and then I've not been able to stand it anymore and I've got to get it out.

So, my boxing was incongruous to me. I don't know why I did it really. Except that I was good at it.

When I came out of the Navy my Dad said he'd get me in at Hull Fishtrades boxing. I made some excuse as to why not to. I didn't like fighting. I don't like getting hit. It hurts. As much as I like being able to do execute the moves, I don't want to fight anybody.

But then, in the Navy, the boxing made me feel wanted and capable and that I had a role that was of value. Losing what it brought me wasn't something I would have wanted to contemplate. But that was to come.

Absent Without Leave

When I was on helicopter controller secondment at Weymouth I put in for PTI – Physical Training Instructor. I was very fit, very motivated, and keen. But I got declined. And it was at that point that my internal decline started with the Navy.

The training to be a PTI is hard, at a place called HMS Temeraire, but I knew I could do it. I'd done all my research; I knew I'd probably struggle on gym and vault floor work but if you're promising they give you extra tuition. There's one PTI per ship, it's a great job, you keep fit for life and I'd specialise in boxing and swimming, I was a good swimmer as well as a boxer.

But the commander I saw, at the air base, said that, because the computers on the ships were new, I was too valuable a resource, with my experience on the ADAWS weapons systems, not to send back to a ship. So, I was declined.

And I took my ball home.

I don't remember the exact feeling. But I remember thinking 'Fuck it. I ain't doing it anymore'. And that was the start of a steady decline for me.

I'd got engaged to a girlfriend in Weymouth, D, while at HMS Osprey and by this time I'd started to decline enough to want a break from the Navy.

I approached D's dad, Frank, who was part of a travelling family, and told him I fancied a bit of time off.

"Come and work with me in the slaughterhouse," he said.

I lasted about two weeks. It is exactly like Silence of the Lambs. They bolt gun lambs, all that sort of thing. It's not nice. I didn't learn to dice or cut up anything, I mainly took skins off, things like that. But it was horrible. Just horrible.

I eventually told Frank I couldn't do it.

"Well...One of my travelling friends has got a fair," he said, "They go away for six months in the summer. Do you want to get on that?"

"Ooh, yeah!"

Obviously my fiancé didn't want me to do it, but she said I could if I wanted. She wasn't super happy about it though. For understandable reasons.

I joined the travelling fair, which went all the way across Dorset for six months. It was me and one other guy in a caravan, you got thirty pounds a week, three square meals a day and you had to work on whichever ride it was. My ride was the speedway.

We got to Swanage which was the first site and the first time the ride was built up. This is extremely hard work – everything weighs a ton. Then the fair inspector comes and inspects the ride.

After the fair inspector had been, Bernard, the owner of the ride came up to me and said:

"Right, I'm off to the pub," it was something like 11am by this point, "This is the lever. Zero is stop. Ten is fast. By the time I come back from the pub, you need to be able to ride this machine at ten."

The ride is made up of cheeseboards making up a big circle, with wooden motorcycles and carriages set in them, and there's a bar at the end of each cheeseboard shaped like an upturned U, with a middle piece in, a bit like a safety bar.

I spent the next two hours, music on, learning to ride this machine. I took to it like a duck to water. I could ride it at ten and I used to dance while the ride was going.

I was very personable, and I was probably the cleanest, smartest fairground person you'd ever seen. So, it was a no-brainer for the women really. Because a lot of women are drawn to fairground people. To have a fairground person who was quite attractive, and I was handsome, and clean, was like double bubble. I had to fight them off.

On the first night Bernard says to me;

"There's a bit of a tradition here. There are these two twins that come, if you give them a free ride; I guarantee they'll give you one."

So, these two blonde twins came, and I gave them their free ride and then ended up leaving with them at the end of the night. They had a big old-fashioned Jaguar, which was their brother's, and I bonked both in the car, one in the front seat, one in the back. And that was just my first night there.

Different small fairs used to meet up. One time this happened I thought I'd go over and look at the Whip. I spoke to the guy at the ride, who knew Bernard and was very friendly, had a pint with him and he let me have a go on the ride.

As I was on there, a couple of locals came over. They grabbed my arm with the pint in it and told me I was going to get sorted (because they didn't like you chatting up their women).

That was the first time I ever had any feeling of camaraderie in the fairground, because quite a lot of fairground lads came over and stood close by.

They didn't have to say anything. They were all obviously mean looking dudes and the locals fucked off.

"Any issues Steve, give us a shout," the fairground lads said, "We'll be there."

The work was incredibly hard. The wedges must have weighed quarter of a ton, each. You get fairground lads who are regulars and just join the fair for certain towns and this lad called John joined us at one point. I was on the pointed end of the wedge and John and somebody else were on the other end. After five or six wedges you couldn't feel your hands. But you had to carry on. But, back then, at that age, you had boundless energy.

If you were going the next morning, then you used to finish the night at 11, and you had to rip the ride down and then you'd be on the road and you were at the next place by 4/5 o'clock.

While he was with the fairground, John, who was a really big, skinny, ugly dude, but a great guy, told me he would teach me something, something that I'd never seen before, and never seen since, and told me that it would absolutely guarantee, if it needed any more guaranteeing, fanny.

"There's only me does this," he said, before showing me his trick.

What we used to do is get up on the upturned U safety bar, one foot up on the middle bar and the other over the top on the middle bar, and we used to stand, facing the direction of the ride, stood upright, ducking under the lights, like a pigeon. The centrifugal force you counterbalance by leaning in. We used to do that as a party trick, me and John.

I think of it now and I think 'How?! How did I do that?' It used to bring, literally, gasps. Because you were risking your life. But I've never, ever seen anybody else do that. Ever. And I don't think I'd see it again, what with health and safety. Bur it really was a crowd puller.

I could jump on and off the ride at full speed without even thinking. You'd spot your gap at 180 degrees to you, as it was coming around, so by the time your gap was twenty yards from you, you were already leaning in. Because that was how to do it, you used to lean in and then – whoosh – and on. It's all about pre-judging where the gap's going to be when you jump on. The centrifugal thing was just a case of balance. But I'd never seen it before, never seen it since.

There wasn't a real reason for jumping on and off it except showing off. When a song came on that I liked I used to get up and dance in the middle, do a bit of Michael Jackson shuffle and a bit of Northern Soul in the middle while the thing's going around. So I used to boogie around, but you can't do that for four or five hours, so every now and then you'd take your money and you'd just jump off, have a fag, have a chat with somebody, chat with the crowd, and then jump back on.

My fiancé kept turning up at random times, as well. She was incredibly jealous. I was never going to marry her, which she probably knew. I'd spot her from 500 yards away, stood behind a fairground ride just watching. But I was never going to marry her.

There was an instance where I was at one place and had met two girls and this other fairground lad, who was a bit rough looking, but a nice guy, asked;

"These two girls... Can I tag along?"

"Yeah, course you can," I said, "If they don't mind."

One of these girls was up for it, bubbly and vivacious. The other one was very quiet. So, he says;

"I want that one! The one that's really up for it!"

"Yeah, alright then." I shrugged.

We went back to their place. As we got to their residence I asked, 'how are we going to get in, because it's a bit...?'

"It's ok, it's a home for the blind," the bubbly one said, "Nobody will see you."

I thought, it can't get any more surreal than that. Nobody will see you because they're blind...Bloody hell. You couldn't make it up.

They were care workers there and lived in a flat at the top of the building.

So, we went upstairs, and the fairground lad went off with his girl and I thought 'I'm going to have a quiet night now' because mine's not said three words all night.

We went into the front room where there was a settee.

"You get settled there," she said, "I'm just going to go and get ready for bed."

"Right, ok then..."

So, I'm lying on the settee and she comes in wearing one of those nightgowns that's buttoned up to the neck, a bit like Victoriana. And I'm thinking 'bloody hell...Well, I'll have a night off then, I suppose...'

She got in the bed and suddenly said, right out of the blue;

"Rip it off me."

"Excuse me?" I said.

"Rip it off me!"

"Wh -?"

"Rip my nightgown off! Rip it off me!"

So, I had a go at ripping it off, half-heartedly, as you do.

"Bite me! Bite my nipples!" she said, I couldn't believe it.

"What?!"

"Bite my nipples!" she kept asking. But I couldn't do it.

Anyway, we got started and I put my hands underneath her, to grab her bum, and said something like 'You've got a really nice bum.'

She then jumped up, leaned over the back of the settee and said;

"Well fuck it then!"

I just thought 'Where's all this come from'. It was like being hit round the head with a hammer.

It was like that Sally Field film, Sybil, about the girl with sixteen different personalities. I just thought, 'Where's she gone?! That quiet demure girl?'

I was wearing a white shirt, and, in the morning, I was covered in scratches and bites. On the way out I was told that my friend had left the night before. I think his had binned him off about ten minutes after she'd got to the room.

I got back to the fairground and this guy was on his ride. He just looked at me;

"What's happened to you?!" he said.

"You won't believe me...."

It just goes to show you can never, ever judge a book by its cover.

There's an unwritten rule that non-travellers don't have relations with travellers. Back in the day, it was total anathema. I never did until about three quarters of the way through the stint. I had enough girls to not need to.

One of the other fairground guys, who looked a bit like Mel Smith but bigger (big, round, muscular, bald; he looked like he could take your head off), had a daughter, who was probably fifteen or sixteen at the time, and she came onto the ride.

Obviously I knew her from around, but she asked if I wanted to come back to the caravan, and it was obvious what for. I remember thinking 'why now?!' but said 'Yeah, alright then'.

"Bernard, I'm just off for a break..."

"Yeah, alright then."

We went back to the caravan, locked the door and started messing around. At that, there was this huge banging at the door.

It was the father.

"I know you're in there!" he shouted.

The girl pulled me close and whispered;

"Don't say I word," she was dead serious, "Because he will kill you."

My blood ran cold, as they say. And my winky disappeared in a flash. I can remember the sinking feeling as I thought 'Oh my God, I'm trapped'. The caravan was literally rocking. And then he went.

I left the caravan and, with the impetuousness of youth, as you do, I thought 'I'll just nip back on the ride. I can't see him anywhere'.

The next day was a Sunday and I stayed in my caravan as long as I could and pretended to be asleep, because I knew what was going to happen.

At some juncture that afternoon he came up to me and grabbed me round the throat.

"If you go near my daughter again," he said, "I will kill you."

I absolutely papped myself.

When I went out, Bernard was there. Bernard was looking at me like my granddad had discovered I'd pissed on his shoes or something. So obviously my days were numbered.

As you might expect, I had to leave, which was sad, really, not to see it through to the end.

After I left, after about six months, I discovered that the MOD had been looking for me the whole time.

I didn't discover at the time the full extent of their efforts but, even as late as when I moved back to Hull, I heard from ex-girlfriends there that they'd had the Ministry of Defence at their house looking for me.

They are thorough. But they couldn't find me. I later discovered that the local regulating branch in Portsmouth had a sweepstake on who was going to get me. And there was quite a lot of money involved.

Anyway, when I got back to Weymouth I said to D;

"I think I'm going to have to give myself in." It had been six months. I didn't have any money.

When I handed myself in, I was on an overpass bridge in Weymouth, on a beautiful sunny day, and went into the phone box and rang the regulating branch.

"It's Steve Utting," I said, "I want to give myself in."

"Are you sure?" they sounded sceptical, "Is it you?"

"Yeah, it's me."

"You're not joking are you?" you could hear the growing excitement, "Because I can get there in half an hour. You promise you'll stay where you are?"

"Yeah, yeah. I'll stay where I am. Course I will."

They'd looked everywhere. They'd been in all my haunts, all my pubs, they'd been all round Hull, they'd looked up all my old girlfriends, and they'd been to my home. They'd been everywhere and couldn't get me.

So, the people that picked me up were cock-a-hoop. They'd won the sweepstake. They'd got me, like I was Mr Big or something.

But it just goes to show you, even when you're a tiny cog in the Royal Navy, they don't let you go.

For going AWOL I got 28 days in the Royal Naval Detention Quarters. It was my second time in there. The Naval Detention Quarters is in HMS Nelson in the middle of Portsmouth. It's exactly like Strangeways prison, the nets, the cells, it's all Victorian.

It's part of my personality that I thrive under order and routine. So, within days I'd settled in. I never liked the lock up because I always felt claustrophobic, but I made myself cope with it. I'd do exercises in my cell after lights out, for two or three hours.

You do a mile and a half run in the morning and then you do a naval fitness test every week. These tests were six exercises; a mile and a half run, a timed shuttle run, as many dips as you can do in a minute on the bar, as many pull ups as you can do, as many squat thrusts as you can do and as many push ups. Six exercises at six hundred points and I scored six hundred points. I could do the mile and a half in, not quite Olympic time, something like just over six minutes, bearing in mind that it was a round course. I used to burn round it. I was good at it and I really liked it, and you used to get to wear a yellow jersey in the morning on the run, if you were top.

At the time, and for who knows how long afterwards, I held the record for the naval fitness test. I always miss that part of my life, being as fit as that. But you move on.

You'd get an hour's time in the wing to sit at a table doing fuck all, just like in Porridge, other than that, the rules were strict. You couldn't put your hands in your pockets, and you had to run everywhere, at double pace. Every time you saw an officer you had to stop what you're doing, give a salute and ask for permission to carry on, and then carry on. They're never spaghetti officers, they're all Chief Petty Officers, normally that are leaving the service, so they're all old salts.

There was this one officer that was called the Screaming Skull. Now they called him this because he looked like a skull with a hat on. He wore his hat with his peak down, right over his nose. How he ever saw anything I don't know.

I'd been there for about two or three of weeks and I was stood about on the wing and, for once, without thinking, I put my hand in my pocket. The Screaming Skull was about ten feet away and he just started screaming at me. And it made me jump.

When somebody makes you jump, certainly with me, it makes you annoyed, and I was fuming.

"Get in my office!" he screamed and then he walked ahead to his office, which was further up the wing.

As I was walking up to it, I was just thinking 'I'm going to fucking do him…'

I used to have those sorts of thoughts, when I got angry, but I usually never actually carried them out, or something stopped it from happening.

So, I went into his office, which was another cell. He was sat behind his desk with a smug expression.

'Right you fucker,' I thought.

And then I closed the door behind me.

This was taboo. He knew then he was in trouble.

"Come on lad, open the door," he realised the danger, "Open the door…"

I must have had that look in my face. I was only 140 pounds dripping wet. But still.

"Come on lad," he'd realised he'd overstepped a mark, "Open the door and we'll talk about this man to man."

And I opened the door.

The tension was diffused enough for us to talk then.

"You made me jump, screaming in my fucking ear," I said, "Apart from damaging my fucking ear drum, you made me jump. It's not necessary."

"There's rules lad – "

"I know," I stood my ground, "And I follow them rules. I'm pretty good in here. But you made me jump. You can't do that."

I didn't get any extra time for that, and I could have. The Screaming skull didn't back down exactly, but he'd realised he'd pushed the wrong button and that it would be best for everybody if we just got on with it.

For my part, the adrenalin had gone, and I do have integrity and I thought 'fair enough, I've made my point'. It was an out for both of us and nothing more was made of it.

The second time I went AWOL I found a job in a factory. I made up a name; I think I called myself Steve Robson. I didn't have any identification papers or anything like that, I was paid cash in hand, I was on the books, but I didn't pay tax or anything like that.

I was just dropping things into a smelting tank mostly. It was menial factory work and I loved it.

I was all dressed in my punk gear, everyone had a laugh on the shop floor, it was different to what I was used to, and I'd never done anything else for years, other than being in the Navy.

I was there for maybe four or five weeks before somebody dobbed me in.

I got a call to the office.

"Steve, there's some people to see you in the office!"

There was no way out apart from that way. As soon as I met them I felt real hostility.

They took me back and straight to see this Commander, whoever he was. He looked me over and said;

"Just stand there and turn around for me, will you."

I did a turn, with my bondage pants and punk gear on.

"What a fucking mess." He said.

"You're a fucking mess." I spat back.

That got to him. You could see the anger.

"Get that man out of here!" he shouted, "And get that shit off him!"

Once I was back inside I got invited to the Captain's office. Once again, it was a cell, like the Screaming Skull's office had been.

"This is the second time you've been in here," the Captain was levelling with me, "Are you working your ticket?"

Working your ticket is the term for performing deliberately badly so the Navy will kick you out.

I remember thinking it over.

"No," I said, pretty certain of what I was saying, "No, I'm not."

"Your record on ship is excellent," he said, "It's when you get in port. Your mind isn't on the ship; it's in your bollocks. And you're off."

"Yeah…" I nodded, "I just…"

I didn't have an answer to that. I knew he was right.

I enjoyed being on the ship when it was at sea, there was no distraction of women, because women were the first thing on my mind – always. And there's a certain stress level that goes with that, even when you're that young, even though you don't realise it as that, but there is, because you're always thinking 'I need to do it'.

On ship, because there were no women on ship then, that pressure was gone, and I used to concentrate on my job. And I was good at my job.

But it wouldn't be long before that would be taken away too.

Locked Up

As I've said already, at HMS Dryad I had been boxing for a while, and successfully. But what I hadn't done was a medical without my contact lenses in.

I've always had issues with my eyesight, but whenever I'd had to take a medical for the boxing I'd worn my contact lenses. On this one occasion I had conjunctivitis so I couldn't wear my contact lenses. I had a fight in three or four weeks, so I needed to take a boxing medical.

I didn't pass it.

The medic shook his head.

"That's it," he said, "No boxing."

And that was it. I couldn't box anymore, for the Navy at least.

I went back to my boxing trainer, Topsy Turner, who had told me I could make a good boxer and told him I'd failed the medical.

"I can't box anymore," I said, "But I still want to come to training."

Topsy made a face.

"You're no good to me," he answered, "That's it. Done."

With hindsight I understood but at the time I was devastated. It was one of the only things I knew I was good at and felt like I was part of the team.

That night I went out and had a drink for the first time in maybe a year. I was drinking Tiger beer at a pub near HMS Dryad in Portsmouth.

I got drunk, not fall down drunk, and went back to the base NAAFI, a big disco/club, and sat on my own. After a while I decided to go and call my then fiancé, who lived in Weymouth.

I went out and called her and, on my way back, feeling a lot better about myself, somebody tripped me up.

I turned around and there were these three field gunners and their partners. If you've seen the Edinburgh Tattoo, Field Gunners are the people who run the gun in bits and put it together. Big boys.

"What did you do that for?" I asked.

My memory of the exact wording of their reply isn't pin prick but their attitude was along the lines of 'Fuck off and do one'.

So, I went to the bar, picked up a tankard glass, smashed it, and the base of it, which was about the size of the bottom of a teacup, I had in my hand. The scars from holding it are still there on my hand to this day.

By the time I went back to the Field Gunners, my recollection of having the glass in my hand was gone, swallowed up by red mist.

The guy that had tripped me, the biggest one, stood up in response to me. And his two friends stood up beside him, one on the left, and one on the right.

It all happened really quickly. The one on the left moved towards me. I chopped him in the throat, and he went down gurgling. At that point his girlfriend started squealing.

The one on the right, who'd not really moved, I turned and kicked him in the nuts. And he went down.

The big one moved towards me and, as he did so, I went to do a temple punch, which is a side punch to the temple, normally a knock down move in karate.

But I had the glass in my hand.

As I banged him on his temple there was an instant spray of blood everywhere.

As he went down, he tried to fall on me to stop me from doing anything else and I started biting his neck to get him off me and give me room to pan him.

I can't give an excuse for it because there isn't an excuse. I wasn't consciously doing anything. It was like auto red mist mode.

In reality, as good as I was at it, fighting frightened me. When I boxed, I was very aggressive, the same with karate. I was very good at form, but I didn't like sparring. Because when I did I was over the top, even to the extent that I would lose control. And that night, in the NAAFI, I lost all control. Completely.

Somebody pulled me off him and I went to the toilets to see to my right ring finger, which was hanging off. The glass bottom had cut deep around my fingers and hand, I was holding it that tight.

Somebody called the Military Police. The MPs came and took me, and him, off in an ambulance to the naval hospital. By that time, he was unconscious in the ambulance. I was still in annoyed mode. When I got to the hospital I wanted to find him and kill him, or at least that was what I said.

They stitched my hand, but somebody had obviously told the guy what I'd done, as it was stitched without any injections or anything. He just said, 'this is going to hurt'. And it did.

For about four weeks afterwards my finger was grey. It smelled; it was awful. I didn't think it was going to take, but thankfully it did. Even now, though, the feeling in it is pretty much just pins and needles.

I made it onto on Police 5, that kind of assault was quite rare at the time, so it was big news. It was also obvious I was going to have a Court Martial and there hadn't been a Court Martial for ages.

While waiting for the Court Martial, I spent a lot of time in detention quarters in a place called HMS Nelson, in the middle of Portsmouth.

As is my wont, I got on with everybody in detention. I was supposed to be on 24/7 watch, because there's nowhere to go, but they let me have the cell door open, I could watch TV, I could do what I wanted, I just got on with everybody.

On the day of the Court Martial I was walked in flanked by ratings with swords. It's all tradition and bullshit.

I had a lawyer representing me, the defence officer, but obviously it was a naval lawyer, so he was part of their set up. And there was no real defence for what I'd done.

It was very much like A Few Good Men, all run internally. I faced a three-man panel, all officers and a prosecuting officer. There were stenographers writing down proceedings and reporters from the press observing.

I looked around for the Field Gunners.

"Where are they?" I asked my lawyer.

"They're not bringing them in," he said, "They're all big guys."

With hindsight, it was obvious why they didn't bring the Field Gunners into the court. Because he was right. They were huge. At that point I was 5'7'' and weighed 140 pounds. Comparing our sizes might lend some credence to the idea of me acting in self-defence, the idea that I was intimidated and felt threatened.

Although that wasn't how I felt. I knew I could defend myself. They'd tripped me up for no good reason and that was what annoyed me more than anything, because there was no need for it.

The court read out the description of what I'd done and, in black and white, it was horrific.

"You used far too much force," they said, "You were aware of how to defend yourself and what you were capable of. You were under the influence of drink…"

It was open and shut. I got the impression they knew what they were going to do, signed, sealed, delivered, just get him in and get him out.

They had witness statements too, saying that, even in the hospital, I was still trying to get him. I don't think I really would have, well…I don't know. But that was what I'd been saying when I was in there.

I didn't try to defend myself. By then I just wanted it over with. I probably never said more than two words through the whole proceedings.

I got charged with Grievous Bodily Harm and given eighteen months in a military corrective training centre – MCTC - and was discharged from the Navy.

After the sentence was read out I threw my cap into the centre of the court.

"I won't need that then." I said.

The response was immediate and furious.

"Take that sailor away!" They shouted. And that was the end of my Court Martial.

I was sent to the military corrective training centre in Colchester. It's made up of four wings; A, B and C wings are Army. A and B are for Army who have done something and are going back to the Army, C Wing is for Army who have done something and are going out and D Wing is for Naval and Air Force who have done something and are leaving the service and going back to civvie street. So, I'm in D Wing.

Your first few weeks (or months with a long sentence) are in a Nissen Hut, shared with several other guys.

I went in and there were loads of Army guys and one other Navy guy in my hut.

The first thing you're asked is 'What are you in for?'.

"I don't want to talk about it..." I said.

"Forget that bullshit!" the response was pretty strong, "We're all in here for the same reason. If you've got eighteen months, what've you done?"

I told them and there was no real shame or pride in it. It was what it was. And that's how I got to know everybody.

I met one other Navy guy that first day, he was Scottish, he was in there for six months for stabbing someone.

It's quite a tough routine in military prison, as you'd imagine. You're up at half past 5, you go for a march, you have your breakfast at 6/6.30, you do certain jobs throughout the day, you march everywhere, and you get just 1,000 calories a day to eat and no more.

But again, it was ordered, so I fell into the routine quite easily. I was still personable too, for the most part, with the odd exception.

I was booked in by Redcaps on that initial day. The main Redcaps were arseholes and I refused to call them Sir.

"You can call me Mr," I told them, "Because I'm not in the Navy anymore."

"You're in the fucking Navy till you leave here!"

"Nah." I wasn't having any of it.

"You'll call me Sir!"

"I fucking won't."

Once I said I wasn't going to do it do it, I couldn't back down. There were people who I would call Sir, but on that initial day, not them. I just thought, 'No way, you fucking Red Cap bastards, am I calling you Sir. First, you're Army and secondly I'm on my way out. Fuck off.'.

There's a stockade there, a prison within a prison in the middle of the camp, which you get as punishment, bread and water, with remission taken off your sentence.

You got so many pence a day, maybe about a pound a week, to spend on baccy or whatever.

In the first couple of weeks I got called into the office of the Captain who ran my wing.

"Ah, Utting," "Sit down lad."

Once again, I was very personable, so I got on with everybody, and I got on with this officer, he was a decent guy.

He put some boots on the table.

"I want you to clean them for me," "Once a week."

"No," I said, "I'm not cleaning your boots."

"Clean my boots," he persisted, "I'll give you a pound a week."

"No, I'm not cleaning your boots," I didn't hide my feelings, "That's wrong."

"It's a tradition," he said, "Somebody out of every wing does it. A pound a week is double what you get normally. What I suggest you do is take the boots into the camp, pay somebody 50p to clean them for you, bring them back to me, I'll give you a pound."

"Ok," I said at last.

I went to an Army guy I quite liked, offered him 50p and he agreed to do it. He used to shine the boots, which I could never do, and I'd deliver them, get a pound and give him 50p.

I always got on with that officer and that relationship would work to my benefit later.

At one point we went out on parade and I came out in my cotton white front. It's much easier to wear a woolly pully, which is also part of naval uniform, but I never used to like wearing them. I was sensitive to them and they used to make me itch.

So, I was in a line-up, with three Navy guys, who I wasn't friends with, but I knew, and thought they were knob ends, and they were all wearing woolly pullies. Like I say, they were easier to put on, just pull them over your head, they're jumpers.

The Army officer came up to me and said;

"Why aren't you wearing a woolly pully?"
"Because it's not regulation uniform." I answered.
"These lot say it is," he nodded at the other Navy guys.

"They're lying," I said. That set things off.

"You fucking...!!" the guys just started effing and blinding "Don't you fucking...!!"

There was no way I was going to wear a jumper, because it was uncomfortable. So, I rode it out.

"No, no," I said, "Check standing orders. Woolly pullies not standard issue. You need to wear a shirt underneath it and it's for when you're on ship, when it's cold. It's a white front other than that."

I successfully stood my ground but that meant I fell out with the other Navy guys. They never did anything. I used to take boxing and karate classes in one of the huts of a night, with a couple of guys that came and took the class with me, and I was in for wounding, so people knew not to mess with me. You just have to brass it out.

After a certain amount of time you get put in a hut in another part of the camp with four people, you get a bit more freedom and you get a job to do.

There was guy in my hut called Steve. Ex-Army. And he'd joined the Army because he wanted to kill people. He got through all the initial training but when it got to the nitty gritty they started to realise what he was about; he took sniper courses and everything. Eventually they realised 'We can't let this guy into the Army because he will kill people'. So, they binned him out. Go figure!

I can't remember what he'd done but he must have done something because it warranted a stay. Anyway, I got on with him like a house on fire.

He taught me to leopard crawl, creeping around without being heard. So, we used to black up with boot polish, as camo, and we'd leopard crawl and break into the kitchens, then we'd open the fridges and eat anything that wasn't nailed down.

On 1,000 calories a day, of course, you were hungry all the time. There was one time we were biting chunks out of big blocks of cheese and squirting squirty cream, filling our mouths with it. We were sick as pigs.

Of course, it was all round the camp, because we'd left bite marks in the cheese. They were going barmy trying to found out who it was. And of course, it was us, blacked up and leopard crawling round the perimeter.

It was funny. We were cackling like Hyenas going around.

When you've been in there for six months you get one half day out in Colchester. You've got to wear your uniform, you've got to wear your hat, and you can't go in any drinking establishments. It's just to get you out of the camp.

Colchester's the training ground for Redcaps, so you get these little baby Redcaps everywhere.

I went out once with a guy called Jock. The first Navy guy I met. He was what everyone thought I was. He was a psycho. He was only a little guy, but he was dangerous. But I really got on with him.

He was quiet. Never said ten words when one would do.

We were out in Colchester, we'd got our coats off, caps off, and we'd already had a couple of sherbets. Then these two baby Redcaps came up to us.

"Put your cap on." They said.

"You can fuck off." Jock answered.

"Put your caps on or we'll arrest you," the Redcaps kept on.

Jock turned to me;

"Follow me," he said and turned away from the Redcaps, "

"There's a dead end around the corner," Jock said, "If they follow us we're going to fucking do them."

We went around the corner and the Redcaps never came in, so they must have twigged.

Later, for one of these parole days Steve says to me;

"My sister and her friend are coming up to see us," he says, "And we're going to Clacton on Sea."

"Right...ok, then." I said.

They came up and met us in Colchester. Steve's sister had a little Volkswagen Beetle, we had fags, and we had beer. I was in the back with his sister's friend and we went off to Clacton, which is the seaside, about 30 miles away, and had a great afternoon.

Either the next day or the day after that I got called to the office of the Captain whose boots I cleaned.

"Come on in Utting. Sit down lad."

I sat down, not thinking anything was up.

"So...Friday afternoon." The Captain said.

"Yes Sir."

"Where were you?"

Bear in mind I was a consummate liar. Lying was always my first line of defence.

"Parole day, Sir," I answered, "So I was in Colchester, Sir. In the centre."

"Colchester in the centre..." he said, "The whole time?"

"Yes Sir."

"Right... So, it wasn't you I saw in the back seat of a Volkswagen Beetle, drinking and smoking, with a rather attractive young girl, on the way out of Colchester."

I paused. I'd been rumbled.

"Erm...it might have been me." I said.

"Where did you go?"

I could see him holding himself back, trying not to show how funny he was finding it all.

"Clacton Sir."

"Clacton?" he said, "So you went to the seaside?"

"Yes sir."

"You do know that you can't go more than half a mile out of the city centre?"

"Yes Sir. It was a lovely day, Sir."

"Right," he said, finally cracking a smile, "Your next answer will denote whether or not you receive any punishment."

"Yes Sir."

"Did you bring," he said slowly and deliberately, "Any rock back?"

And, of course, I hadn't.

"No Sir."

"Right so we need to punish you then, don't we...?"

I think I did boot duty for nothing for a month, or a few days of number nines. But I could have got stockade for that. Twenty-eight days. Easy.

So that relationship we had developed initially, through cleaning his boots, led to that outcome, where he found it funny and I didn't get punished, not all that badly anyway.

How we got the money for that Clacton trip is a story on its own.

Steve and I used to work on the pig farm. The camp ran their own pig farm and it used to generate money for the farm. It was quite a good job, because you were outdoors, although it could be quite dangerous, because pigs can be nasty fuckers.

Back in the day, before everything was computerised, in the entrance to the office section of the pig farm was a great big chalk board with all the numbers of all the pigs that were in there at the time. So, you had so many sows, so many boars, so many babies, so many wieners, so many of all the different weights and ages, all written up on the board.

One time, while me and Steve were out in Colchester, in a pub, a guy sat next to us.

"You boys are obviously MCTC," he said.

"Yeah,"

"What do you do there?"

"Work on the pig farm." We answered.

"Perfect!" he grinned, "I'm after a couple of pigs."

"Really?"

"Yeah, just babies," he said, "I'll give you twelve pounds a pig."

Twelve pounds a pig! Winner, winner.

We agreed to meet him at one of the perimeters to the camp, behind the woods.

So...night-time. Black up. Leopard crawl. Pigs in a sack – squealing like Billy-O. Rubbed out 25 on the chalkboard, put 23. To the fence. Give him the sack. Twelve quid each. Easy money.

It was so funny. We were manically laughing as we were running through the woods trying to keep these pigs quiet as they were squealing away in the sack.

And, obviously, that £12 took us to Clacton.

While I was at MCTC a creative side of my life started. I met a guy there called Billy Pickup, who told me he used to be the guitarist with the Skids, before they made it big. I've since learned he wasn't, from someone I met on the pub music circuit whose friend was a cousin of Richard Jobson, the lead singer of the Skids. He's got a Skids appreciation society and I often joke I'm not joining it unless Billy Pickup's in it.

But Billy was a great guitarist. I met him during the four-man hut stage of my sentence, and he had a guitar in the hut with him. He could play anything. One time he played me something and I asked him what it was.

"That's one of mine," he said, "I wrote it."

"Wow!" I was amazed, "I write poetry."

"A poem's just a song without music," Billy said, "Let me see what you've done."

I showed him it.

"That could be a song," he said, "Have you got any idea of a tune?"

And he just played it.

"Wow! I need to learn how to do that!"

So, he taught me some chords.

We made a tape, which I've still got now, of six songs. I played a matchbox as a drum and made my first efforts at singing, which sound poor now, because I can hear myself straining, back then I didn't know how to breathe properly.

We sent it off to record companies.

We never had any joy with it. We got one letter back from United Artists...

Dear Mr Utting, thank you for your tape and manuscript, which we have listened to with great interest, and while we do not find them quite strong enough for inclusion in the United Artists catalogue, we'd be very interested to hear anything else you've done.

I know now that that's a stock letter. But then we got it back and thought 'Fucking hell! United Artists!'.

Although I didn't know it at the time, my song writing was a cathartic exercise. Everything I write, barring a couple of throwaway songs, are all autobiographical and in MCTC was where I wrote *Endless*.

In the end I left MCTC after doing around fourteen months, rather than the full eighteen I was sentenced to, leaving just before the Falklands War, where I might have been serving on the Coventry, if it weren't for fate.

On leaving, when I got my naval documents, I noticed they hadn't cut the corner off. All Naval records had, on the top corner, 'this corner to be cut off if discharged dishonourably' and, at the time, some employers would ask to see your naval records so that missing corner could have really affected my ability to get a job.

My Dad, who was a practical joker in his own way, doctored my naval documents. On the back, where it showed my eighteen-month sentence, he changed it to some other naval service and signed it 'Commanding Officer – Jeremy Beadle'.

I never noticed that for years, and when I did I thought it was funny.

Only one employer ever asked to see my naval record though, and that was Debenhams. They just took them and handed them back. No worries.

After the Navy

I moved back to Hessle after the end of my sentence. To start with, I slept in the caravan in my Mum and Dad's garden. I just couldn't integrate myself back into that world. It was back to normal in my relationship as far as my Mum and Dad were concerned, but it was more like a boarding house to me.

After a long time in the Navy, and barely visiting Hessle during that whole time, I was a bit of a curiosity. Also, due to my chameleon-like nature, where I pick up the accents of people around me, I'd developed a southern twang, which was quite unusual in Hessle. In hindsight, I probably sounded like a twat.

I met this girl called Valerie, who was Nigerian. Her skin was incredibly dark, blue black, and incredibly soft. She was gorgeous.

On our first night together, she went to bed upstairs and then left me to go to bed downstairs, then did the old trick of coming down half an hour later and inviting me to join her.

"Do you know, that was really good," she said afterwards.

"Well thank you very much…" it wasn't the first time I'd been complimented.

"Yeah, do you know what was good about it?" she continued, "most of my other boyfriends had big cocks and you haven't, so it didn't hurt me."

"Oh…err…thanks…"

Thankful for small mercies. She normally dated big black men but my cheeky chappy grin got me in there.

I remember getting up in the morning and thinking 'bloody hell! That's painful!' and when I looked, I find tiny cuts on the shaft of my penis.

When I went to the doctor, he told me they probably cuts from her pubic hair.

After we'd been going out for a while, I decided to introduce her to my Mum and Dad. I told my Dad on the phone I was planning to bring Valerie to see them.

"Hmm.... I don't think your mother's going to like that," he said. It was clear he was referring to the colour of her skin.

I never thought of my Mum as racist before that. Why would I?

But I said we'd get her some chocolates or something to help soften the blow. I told Valerie what Mum's favourite chocolates were. Although I wasn't entirely honest.

A day or two later we arrived at Mum and Dad's.

"Mum, this is Valerie," Mum was uncomfortable. I could see her just keeping it together.

And then Valerie handed over the box of chocolates.

"Here you are Mrs Utting. I know these are your favourite.

It was a box of Black Magic.

I looked over at Dad and he was obviously finding it funny.

"Oh...thanks very much," Mum took them, and Dad clearly got the joke, but Mum didn't speak to me for days afterwards.

After I left her, Valerie became a lesbian. I don't know what that means!

During that time, I had a few other dalliances. I had a relationship with a couple of half-caste sisters as well, one after the other. They worked for an antiques dealer and I used to go around there when he went away on business, for reasons you can imagine.

But I also learned something about Dad's sex life. I can't remember now if this was when I'd moved back, or one of the few visits I made to Hessle while I was in the Navy, but there was one-time Dad said he wanted to take me the pub.

"Where are we going?"

Dad named the pub and I could tell something was up.

"We don't normally go there?" I said, surprised.

"I want you to meet somebody."

My Dad. Wanting me to meet somebody. That wasn't normal.

When we got there, he pointed to a woman at the bar, about 22 years old.

"That girl at the bar," he said, "My secretary..."

"Ok..."

"She's my girlfriend."

"Right...ok." I didn't know what to say.

At the time I didn't think that much of it, because him doing that was nothing compared to what I'd done. But as the years went by, I've wondered, 'Why did he tell me that?'.

I put this in my letter to my mother, that I wrote after Dad died, telling her that he unloaded that on me, either to show off, or because he had to tell somebody. But he told me and told me to keep it secret from my Mum while she was at home with the kids. That information was one fact alongside a lot of other painful things that I put in that letter. But that was much later.

After a while Mum and Dad moved to Swanland, a new build estate, with what would now be million-pound houses, not far from Hessle. Dad took me up to see the house before he moved in and I felt bad.

"I've worked all my life for this," he said proudly, looking at his house and the estate around it, "I'm here."

I just had to bite my tongue. There was nothing I could say. I didn't like it.

While they were living there with them, I got work nearby. There was a mink farm in Swanland, which you only heard about through word of mouth, and I worked there for their mink season, just before Christmas, skinning them.

Minks are like skunks. You cut a mink and you get that smell all over you. I had to take my clothes off and keep them in the garage and shower outside with a hosepipe. I got a hundred quid, cash in hand, but the work was grim.

The guy who killed them used to snap their necks and, if his hands got swollen up, after doing 400 or 500 minks, he used to not kill them. I'd put minks in my clips sometimes, to start cutting them, and found they were still alive. It really was grim.

The owner had two dogs. One was a house dog, and one was a Jack Russell called Evil-Eyes. It was about as wide as it was long, and the owner never used to feed it. It was there to kill any minks that got out because, if any minks got out in Swanland and got to the pond and killed any of the swans, he would have been closed down straight away. People didn't like him there as it was.

It really was an evil looking dog. I'd be sat at the bench, with a pile of minks in front of me, and Evil-Eyes would come in and jump up on the bench and start growling at the pile of minks. He'd slowly close in on the pile, growling all the time, and get one and then slowly back away with the mink and then go off and scoffle it somewhere.

If the owner ever came in at the time, he would shout, in his surprisingly posh accent;

"Evil-Eyes! Evil-Eyes, get off there!"

He wouldn't ever go near the dog though, because he knew it would rip his arm off.

One afternoon Evil-Eyes followed me home. As he followed me, he went into one of the houses along the way where an Alsatian lived and came back out with a bone. The Alsatian was in there but never went anywhere near Evil-Eyes.

Carrying the bone in his mouth, and the bone was about four times bigger than Evil-Eyes, he followed me the rest of the way home and settled down in the front garden.

"Stephen," My Mum came to me, very concerned, "There's a dog outside and he looks really scary. Whose is it?"

"That's Evil-Eyes." I tried to set her at ease.

But of course, it didn't work. Everybody was too scared to leave the house. I took him some water in the end and at some point, he must have gone back to the mink farm. He wasn't nasty, he just wasn't looked after.

Not long after this I moved to Scunthorpe, and it was in Scunthorpe I met my one and only nymphomaniac, who I went out with for about 6 months.

She was plainly attractive, by which I mean she wasn't a great beauty, but she had a fantastic rack and a great bum. She was quite big, but she was statuesque with it, almost Amazonian.

The first time we did anything I gave her my usual line 'Whatever you want to do, I'll do it'. She responded by taking my bits and rubbing them all over her face, like she'd been six years in the desert without water. It was obviously something she'd not done before, something repressed, and it was like a release for her.

As she was doing it I was thinking 'Fucking hell!'. Winner, winner! She was absolutely mad for it.
After that the floodgates opened.
We used to do it front of mirrors, she even used to like taping it, just for the sound of us having sex. Everything I could think of, we did. She'd cum within five minutes. Then want to do it again. It was incredible. Non-stop.
Every time I looked at her I wanted her. She was all woman. Every time I saw her I couldn't stop looking at her crotch, my eyes were just drawn there immediately. I couldn't stop thinking about doing it.
In the end it got too much. I got fed up. I was doing stuff that you couldn't imagine, well…you could if you had to. We'd tried every position, anything we could just to get that little bit deeper.
But eventually I'd done everything I could think of to do. I've slapped her round the face with it, I've done every position, and you still want that high. And I've got a right imagination, and she did too, but in the end I couldn't think of anything else to do. It was frustrating me, because I couldn't get that buzz any more.
I binned her and within a week I was thinking 'Fuck! What have I done?!'.

And that was my one and only nymphomaniac.

Later, I got a job as the bar manager at the Crest Hotel, in North Ferriby, just outside Hull (the place where I met James Coburn at that wedding).
While I was working at the Crest Hotel was where I met my wife. She was working as a silver service waitress in the restaurant.
She was the opposite of everyone I'd ever had a relationship with. She was quiet and unassuming, and she was blonde, and I'd always wanted blonde daughters. No Son for me – go figure.
I think I picked her, using certain parameters – not romantic at all. I loved her but I wasn't in love with her in the way I would be with H, the girl I met in my 40s. My wife never refused me anything, and

she hadn't a bad bone in her body, but our relationship wasn't passionate. When I came home the dog was all over me and my wife just said hello. It was at times, more a marriage of convenience.

It didn't excite me, but I was looking for stability. She was what I needed in my life at that time.

We courted for a couple of years and then got married. On my birthday – no forgetting anniversaries for me! We had 2 girls, both blondes – exactly what I wanted, and they are my proudest achievement.

Sadly, life at home with my family also had its down times. I was struggling mentally with quite a few issues and it was difficult for my children to understand. Again, it's a guilt I carry to this day and I'm forever grateful to them that we have a great relationship now.

It was during this time that I had my worst episode of illness. It is almost impossible to describe to someone who has never suffered, the incredible feeling of emptiness that real depression brings. I couldn't get out of bed, I couldn't interact with people, I hid at work and so my job suffered. It got to the point where I went to the doctors for an appointment and after being told there was one available in around ten days' time, I went back home and stood in my living room for an hour, not moving, hardly taking a breath. I then rang the doctors and told them if I didn't get a call back from a doctor in the next minute – I would kill myself. Matter of fact. I got the call and went back up to speak to a doctor. It was the first time I had ever unloaded my thoughts and the sense of relief was immeasurable. It was also the first time I had cried for a while – and that felt good too.

*

In 1984 my Dad passed away. This was a massive shock and the start of extreme health anxiety and depression for me.

My sisters were the apple of my Dad's eye. We all took it hard, but they got on with their lives. I went to ratshit. As much as it was painful under him, nobody could say a bad word about him. I'd built him up to this massive figure. And he was gone.

So, I started to have serious health anxiety. I even thought I was going to have a heart attack if I walked too fast. I used to need my wife to sleep on my chest, to listen in case my heart stopped. And if you think about it, what would she have been able to do? But I couldn't sleep any other way. I put my wife through murder really.

To sleep, I needed something wrapped round my core, to protect that part of me.

It was bad. I was on an old school drug called amitriptyline, and I was on six of those a day.

I remember going to see the chemist, (and I would get my amitriptyline's in hundreds), and his reaction to my prescription.

There's a scene in the old Stephen King *It* film where the hypochondriac lad goes to the pharmacist, who tries to explain to him that he didn't need the placebos he'd been taking.

"No! I'm ill! My mama says I'm ill!"

And I was like that. On this visit to the chemists he came out and said;

"You don't need to be taking these do you son?" he looked really concerned, I was 22 years old, with big panda eyes from the effects of the drugs, "Six a day. These aren't good."

I remember just thinking 'Just give me them! I need them!'.

And at the time I really did. I was dependent on them to get me through the day. At one time I was even put on Mellaril, the *One Flew Over the Cuckoo's Nest* drug. It knocked me out. I was like a zombie.

I remember going to the doctors and him saying;

"Are you worried?"

"...I'm not fucking worried about anything..." I said, "...I can't speak..."

"Slowed you down though, hasn't it?" he said.

".... Phew...I...Yeah...No.... I can't....I can't be on Mellaril..."

I was also in the psychiatric hospital, De La Pole, for eighteen months, as an outpatient. Growing up as a kid, that was the place that would be thrown about as a looney bin - '*You're going to De La Pole!*'. And then I was there.

That was where I realised the difference between a psychiatrist and a doctor, a psychiatrist can prescribe you drugs as well as look at your mind. I was eighteen months an outpatient there, as I say, and got weaned off the drugs, which I managed well – six a day, five a day, four a day...until I didn't need them anymore. The health anxiety's never left me, it's just at a different level.

It took a lot of therapy to take my Dad off the pedestal that had triggered all this.

One of my first therapists, years later, asked me about my Dad, right at the outset. She must have known somehow.

"Don't say owt about my Dad!" I was almost aggressive at her even bringing him up as if he might have been the problem, talking about him like he'd been God on Earth. Just before he died, he'd spent a lot of time with me, showing me more attention than he ever had.

But she saw through that;

"What has this man, that you've put on a pedestal, done for you Stephen?" she asked.

I thought about it, trying to come up with a response, trying to explain why he was so deserving of that high esteem.

But I couldn't think of anything.

"So why is he there then?" she said, "This man that you're putting on a pedestal, you can't think of anything that he's actually done for you that you would be able to remember. You need to stop feeling guilty, Stephen. You're a successful manager and you've done that yourself."

I wrote a song, relatively recently, called Ripple In The Self, which is about narcissism. It's got the line 'the beast rises from behind the façade of fatherhood' and that's how, in later life, I remembered him. He had his dad mask on but, just behind it, was something nasty. He frightened me. I always thought perception was reality and I often used this assumption to answer my inner angst. Even now, there is always the idea that I could be wrong about my childhood – but how would I know?

After he died, at just 44, part of me thought it was a bad thing he'd died early because he'd escaped me giving him what he deserved, what he'd made me. It's an awful thought to have, because he died so young, and I felt guilty about having it for years. The mind is a funny thing – perception, reality. Am I right or am I wrong? Is it me or is it them?

Things obviously changed for Mum once he died. Mum worshipped him but, by the same token, because she was totally subservient to him, once he died Mum had to sort her life out. As much as she loved him, she had sense of freedom once he was gone, she became very independent. She would never have said that, and maybe it's just my perception. It's a difficult thing to put into words. I guess I mean, she *survived*.

But soon after his death, I was only full of bitter feelings about him and her. I wrote her a letter, in my mid-twenties. I put everything in it that I remembered, from my perspective, about Dad, about how he'd dominated us all. (Me).

It was all about my Dad, although the anger really was aimed at my Mum. I asked her 'Why do you think I used to punch the wall instead of punching you? Because you made my life a fucking misery. But Dad made everyone's life a misery. (Mine). And you all loved him to the moon and back'.

I told her a lot of things she'd never heard before, or maybe things she preferred to not be aware of. I told her about when Dad took me to see his girlfriend and swore me to secrecy, I told her that I remembered when Dad threw a suitcase on the floor and told her to get out and then, a while later, after crawling upstairs drunk, shouted down to her to "Get up here where you belong".

I can't remember what my issues were that brought me to that letter, but I was obviously hurting. And it must have been a painful letter for her to read.

My youngest sister, W, who was 12 when Dad died, has never forgiven me. She won't speak to me even now. I also used to have a close relationship with my Aunty Helen (she was the person I was staying overnight with the night I lost my virginity) but she wrote to me after a previous letter telling me I shouldn't be saying what I'm saying. I wrote to Mum telling her that Helen 'should keep her fucking nose out. She's no angel'. And I've not spoken to her since either.

My Mum's spoken to me plenty of times since, we still have a relationship. She's been to my house once in 30 years. I sometimes feel, in my weaker moments, like she only sees me because she feels guilty, as an act of penance or punishment because she knows I'm right. Again, for me, perception was reality.

But even before the letter she would never visit. She's been to my house once in thirty years, as I recall. With my children growing up she never babysat them once. If I want to see her, it's always me that must drive down the motorway to visit, which I do every so often when I feel a pang of guilt. Otherwise I don't see anybody.
She's surrounded by her kids who she loves. Why does she need me? That's what I assume.

She's often denied that I had a painful childhood. But I've told her she can't deny what I believe.

I accept we all see things differently from different perspectives. There's been no response from my Hull family about my announcements that I'm writing a book and I think that's for one reason and one reason only. They know what's going to be in it.

They're not wallflowers, all my sisters are strong-willed but not one of them has asked about what is going to be in it. But they all have the opportunity to not read it, I guess.

This book, like that letter, is my perspective. I'm sure there were lots of times in my childhood where I wasn't given grief, but those are few and far between in my memory. The things that I remember are the things that I think have shaped my personality. And the longer it goes on the more convinced I am that you can't have one without the other; I wouldn't have the feelings I do about my past if my past hadn't have been full of the kind of events that would shape those feelings.

Of course, I have happy memories – xmas mornings, family holidays, school holidays and playing with my friends from morning till night – rushing in to snatch a quick bite, then back out to carry on. And I remember the one time I hugged my dad. It was in the pub the last time I saw him before he passed away. He had beaten me at pool (he usually did, and I was normally a poor loser) and I don't know why but I told him I never minded losing to him and hugged him. I remember how he smelled, cigarettes, beer, aftershave and *dad*.

He told me that night that he had been having pain and numbness down his arms and I told him to go to the docs. I never saw him again and I felt huge guilt for years. I thought he was invincible – what did I know?

From the Ship to the Stage

Not long after I'd moved back to Hessle, I started having driving lessons. One day I asked to book the next lesson for the coming Saturday with my instructor;
"I can't that day," he said. "I'm up at the new theatre. Half a Sixpence."
"Oh right," I wasn't overly curious, but I asked anyway, "Who's in that then?"
"I am," he said, "I'm Half a Sixpence. I'm Arthur. I'm playing the Tommy Steele character."
"Really?" I was amazed, "At the Hull new theatre? How do I get into that?"
"Just come and audition," he said, "In front of the committee. If you're any good, you're in. We do plays, all that sort of thing."
So, I went to audition, for Hessle Amateur Operatic and Dramatic Society, and I made it in.
It was a new world to me. Believe it or not there aren't many young males in those sorts of companies, but it's full of young girls. I just thought 'why are there no guys? Look at all the fanny!', although I didn't go mad on that, because it was enough for me to just be there.
Ultimately being in this company would be the only thing I missed about living in Hull. I played character parts in Death of a Salesman and a couple of parts in the musical Brigadoon, as well as the lead role in Play it Again Sam.
Brigadoon was a pretty dour musical, but I made something of it for myself by making Frank the bartender comedic. I got a telling off, but I made 2,000 people laugh.
It's near the end and you've got Tommy Albright, the main character, who's been to this mythical land, reminiscing in a New York bar. I'm the barman and my brief is to polish the glasses in the background.

As Tommy Albright finished the end of his soliloquy the choir starts singing "Brigadoon... Brigadoon...." and the lighting goes all dim and ethereal and I decided to give it the old double take, as if I was trying to find out where the singing was coming from. I knew I shouldn't, but the audience then started tittering and laughing and that just egged me on to do it more.

I came off stage and Geoff the director was there;
"Come here!" he said.
"What is it Geoff?" I played innocent.
"Don't! Don't you scene steal again! Bad!!" he said, "It's not supposed to be funny. It's supposed to be mystical!"
"They laughed though, didn't they?"
"It's not funny!" he was laughing too though, "Don't do it again!"

Talking of scene stealing, I've got a story about one of the company's leading lights, Richard. He had a beautiful voice, good looking guy, great actor. Every lead role that came up that demanded skill, Richard was there. My wife loved him. He was one of the few people that you thought if he wanted to go on to do something he could. The other guy I thought the same of, Ben, went on to work with Cilla Black in the West end.

So, me and Richard were both in South Pacific. I played Stew Pot because I was the only member of the company who could do a cartwheel, and Richard was playing the wheeler-dealer, Bilko character.

There's a scene towards the end where they've all got to get to the ship, which we were both in. Richard took me to one side and said;
"There's a part where we've got to say 'Get to the ship, marines. And we'll be right at the back of the stage." He started, "But we're not going to do that. We're going to chase the spotlight. I'm going to put my arm on your shoulder and we're going to walk to the front of the stage and give it some staring out to sea shit."
"But what...?" I protested.
"Stick with me," he grinned.

So that's what we did. It's a long walk from the back of the stage to the front and we were hamming it up the whole way. 'Is that the last of them?'

We got off stage and I don't remember who the director was, but he was going apeshit. Richard was laughing his head off.

"Every time, Steve," Richard said to me, "Get that spotlight and make sure it stays on you. Get your face out there."

We did a musical every year at Hull New Theatre and South Pacific was the one for that year. It was always a professional, proper show. One of the only amateur companies ever to do a full public run. It cost us 20 grand to put each show on and we used to aim to break even.

In the same year we did South Pacific I was also in a play, Play it Again Sam. At that year's awards dinner I remember being sat thinking the two leads in South Pacific were well deserving of the win.

For the category of Best Character Performance, I listened as the winner's performance was being described.

"This guy was manic but in the right way…"

And I was thinking, 'that sounds a bit like me that does…'

"He carried the show for four nights." I was in a Woody Allen play, Play it Again Sam, on stage for the whole two hours, with reams and reams of lines in an American accent.

"What a superb performance…" by this time my wife was in tears, "Come to the stage Steve Utting!"

There are 2,000 members of that society, 500 working members, youth, adults, musicals, plays. So, to win it, out of all that competition, was really something.

In that final year I also got voted onto the committee and, at the time, I was the youngest ever member. The committee was always made up of teachers and lawyers, professionals, and although winning that award and being voted onto the committee were big deals for me, I still felt like a bit of rough.

I was a little fish in a big pond. I never felt like I fitted, I always felt like I had to justify myself.

But when I had to leave Hull, the company was the only thing I missed. Again, it was that acceptance that I got from it, I was a valued member of the company, youngest ever member of the committee, winning a best character performance award, and when I left, I missed it bitterly.

I knew I was due to leave at that awards dinner and, at the table that night, I made a comment.

"I'm best off out," I said, or something along those lines, "I won't miss it. Course I won't."

I know now I was saying that as a defence, so I didn't get emotional. But it wasn't taken that way and I've often regretted saying it.

I saw an advert in the paper for a theatre company in Matlock called Millstone Grit. I read for it and I got accepted. The first play I did I think I did 6 parts and as it was a professional company, got paid for it.

After that we did theatre for education, touring around inner-city schools, doing theatre workshops, condensed versions of Shakespeare with questions before and after, all sorts. I loved it.

Off the back of that work I was able to get an equity card. An equity card is a bit of a catch 22 – you can't get professional work unless you've got an equity card and you can't get an equity card unless you've done professional work. But the work I did for Millstone Grit gave me the minimum of six paid engagements that you need to get an equity card. And having an equity card then allowed me to get work as an extra.

I did all sorts as an extra; Dalziel and Pascoe, Peak Practice and the lead role in an episode of 999, the emergency/disaster re-enactment show with Michael Buerke. I was paid handsomely for that. The pay from that show bought me my second car.

The 999 shoot was in Norwich for five days, and my character's accident involved getting impaled on metal rods.

I had a great time, slept with the production assistant, and learned how the BBC's credit cards got vastly abused.

It was the last series they did, and the biggest budget episode. I even got a photo and actor credit in the TV Times and TV Quick, and the actors never normally got a credit. I think this was because of how well I got on with the crew.

I got on with the crew partly because I'd got my wallet out. They said at the bar that I never had to pay anything, but I insisted.

"I will buy my own drink," I said, "I'll buy a round. I like you guys."

The crew also liked me because, as well as being prepared to pay my way, I was open and honest. Most of the actors they got to work with were up their own arses – their words, not mine – I was just happy to be there.

I met the executive producer who'd insisted on coming down specifically to see the first days filming and he was sat opposite me at dinner. I introduced myself.

"Hi, I'm Steve!"

"Oh, I'm Steve as well!" he said.

"And what do you do?" I asked.

"I'm executive producer." He answered.

I'd had about four pints.

"Yeah?" I persisted, "What do you do for that then?"

The running assistant kicked me under the table.

"Oh...well... I propose how the show should go."

"Well, he does that," I pointed at Roy, the director.

"Yes," he answered, "Exactly. I executive produce that."

"Yeah. But what do you do?"

"Er..." he was starting to get a bit rattled by now, "It's hard to explain really..."

And I thought, 'I know what you do, you take a lot of money for doing fuck all...'

Obviously, somebody then changed the conversation. I didn't mean to give him a hard time. He must have done something, but I wanted him to explain it to me.

It didn't damage my career at all though. That crew asked me back for a different show as a doorman/bouncer. But when Phoenix casting called to tell me that Roy had asked me back, they told me they had to turn it down.

"Why?!" I was gutted.

"The doorman's twenty stone," they said, "It's supposed to be lookie-likie, as near as we can. We can't pad you up for twenty stone." I could probably do it without much padding now though!

When I was forty-two, I met the other love of my life, H. She was 18 and it was like having a second go at my teenage years. We went all in and for the first 6 or 7 years, it was great. Her mum wanted nothing to do with me at first – cos I was a lot older than her daughter, but her dad and I got on well. He knew I was serious, and I promised him I would look after her and I did. After a while, her mum came around and I got a telling off if I never showed for Sunday lunch.

I convinced myself for ages after that it was my decision to leave her, because that made it easier to live with. The reality is that she cheated on me. Just the once. But it devastated me. She'd done the only thing guaranteed to destroy the relationship.

I remember when she told me, despite living in each other's pockets and sharing everything – thinking there were huge spaces of nothing between us. Gaps which I never knew existed.

Bearing in mind I'd done it myself, although not to her, it was the worst thing in the world that anyone could do to me. I'd never had it done to me. Ever. I thought for a long time and still do on the odd occasion, that after all I had done in my life, maybe I deserved it. About time the shoe was on the other foot and all that.

She was the love of my life. I gave her everything. I put her through her degree and masters, I put her through her teacher training, I got her her first car, took her on her first holidays abroad. I gave her everything. I loved her to bits. And she fucked me over, for absolutely no reason.

After she told me she asked to marry me. I don't know why. Maybe to calm troubled waters. But for the next six months, and she stayed with me for six months, I made her life an absolute misery.

She tried everything to try to make it better. We went on holiday to Cornwall and it was a good holiday because we were away from everything. But the minute we got over the county line a cloud came over me and I made her life a living hell.

For the six months after she told me and before she decided she couldn't live with me anymore, I had a suicide kit in the boot of my car; a bottle of vodka, a hosepipe and gaffa tape. I was a right mess and couldn't deal with the betrayal – or the constant imaginings of what she had done. But eventually she left.

I came home from karate one night and, when I got in, she was gone.

I got all my pills out, a hundred pills ready to go. Luckily her mother came around while I was in the toilet and threw them all in her purse. When I came out, she took me to her house.

Her Mum and Dad really liked me, because I'd saved their daughter from drink and drugs when she was 18 and on a slippery slope.

"You've made H what she is," her Dad said, "I can't believe what she's done to you. She always said to me, 'the one good thing about working at W….. is that I met the man I'm going to spend the rest of my life with.'"

So, it shocked her parents, to me it was a blow. And one that mentally I couldn't cope with.

In the end I had to commit myself.

I genuinely believed I would have harmed somebody. I believed I would have harmed her family, who loved me, who'd never done anything to me, just because I couldn't get to H. I didn't know where she was. I told the crisis team when they arrived.

"I think I might harm them," I said, "I think I'm going to harm them because I can't get to her."

My kids were there, all crying.

"Will he do it?" the team asked them.

"I think he will…"

"You've got a choice," the crisis team turned to me, "You can commit yourself or we can commit you. If we commit you, you might not get out, till we say. If you commit yourself then you can still get out when you choose." (Not entirely true, as it turned out).

"I'll commit myself then." I whispered.

I look back on this episode and feel I was weak and soft and a self-centred twat. But you can't change what you are, what you feel.

I remember being in that moment and thinking that the world was ending, and I couldn't stop it.

And so, I went in and it really was like *One Flew Over the Cuckoo's Nest*. Within two days I knew, without even looking at a clock, when my medication was due.

I just stayed on my bed in my bedroom for the first two weeks. The staff came and said to me, 'why don't you come and sit in the lounge?'

"Because they're all fucking mad!" I said, "I don't want to go in there! Why would I want to waste time with them?"

So, I didn't leave my room. And I wasn't eating either. I could eat maybe a spoonful of yoghurt a day. From the time she told me, to the time I got out, I lost four stone, my body just eating itself.

For the first week I was under suicide watch, so was under constant supervision. If I needed to take a dump there'd be somebody sat just a couple of feet away watching me.

After two weeks I had my first interview. I thought I was about to leave to and I told them so.

"No, you're not." They said.

"What?!"

"You'll get out when we say you go out," they said, "You're not ready."

It was like being in jail. I thought 'what if this is my life now? What if I never get out?'

H's father, P, came to visit me while I was in there.

After the night she did what she did, when she didn't come home, I'd gone around P's.

"It won't be what you think," he'd said back then, "I know her."

I brought those words back when he visited me.

"You don't her P, do you? Unprotected sex with someone she met in a nightclub. You don't know her." I really hurt him. I hurt them all, with my words.

By then I'd gone. The lights were on but...

"I've got a letter from her." he said.

"You can burn that fucker."

144

"In six months', time we'll all meet up and chat." He was obviously offering me some crumbs of comfort, but I was having none of it.

"No, we won't," I said, "I'll never forget. Never forgive. Ever."

At first, I used to have real moments of sadness and melancholy which lasted for a few years but after being an ocean liner, she is now just a speck on my horizon.

My sisters came and visited me while I was there too. And I'd cut them all dead. But my daughter Samantha, my eldest and my rock, had rung them and said 'Whatever he's said, whatever he's done, he's not in a good place. Do you want to see him?'

And I wasn't in a good place. I was like a skeleton.

When they visited, my sisters were all crying. By then, I was cried out. I was just empty, like a husk. I think being generally mentally unstable, made it hard to cope with what was just another life issue, really.

I finally came out after about six weeks. It was at the weekend and I came out under my daughter's cognisance to the house me and H had had together.

I had a fire sale, I sold everything to my neighbours, and it was the house that Ikea built - it had everything, big gas range barbecues, a couple of lawnmowers, plastic garden sheds, all sorts. The only positive was that I'd paid everything in advance so with all the money I got back from the Council Tax and the electric and selling the house stuff, I had about three grand and that sorted me out for the move to Doncaster.

My daughter had moved there six months previously and encouraged me to come and see what I thought of it. I started by living on the top floor of her three-story house and initially found it hard to cope.

I never thought I could live on my own. I remember ringing my Mum, and I hardly ever phone my Mum, and told her I didn't think I could do it.

"I felt that way when your Dad went," she said, "But believe me, the sun will shine again. I'm telling you."

I've told myself that the reason for not trying to get in any relationships is that I'll never find another H; twenty-five years my junior, clever, beautiful. But the real reason is, I don't want to let anybody in anymore. Not to be hurt like that again. I don't want to risk letting anyone into my life.

It was only when I moved out to live on my own, in my own flat, and all I did was work, go home, and sit on my own, that the anxiety really began to set in.

It was at that time that my real sister, Dawn, got cancer.

She was the sister who had stayed with my real Mum when she and my Dad separated, and I went to live with him. She'd always written to me and I'd always been lax in writing back. I felt guilty about it, but relationships are difficult for me. I always thought 'what do I want to write for if I don't know what to write?'

I remember having the phone conversation with her.

"How are you with it all?" I didn't really know what to ask.

"What do you think?" She said. She was bitter. Not at me, at the disease. She had a young family and the cancer had spread.

I remember getting off the phone and feeling bad for *me*.

'What if I get what she's got?'

Of course, thinking like that produces its own guilt but that was my over-riding thought, 'What if it happens to me?' I know it's not hereditary, but she'd died of cancer, my Dad had died of a heart attack, what if I'm next? Listening to her voice on the phone, having that edge of bitterness in it, made it a hundred times worse. It was then that I started fretting and checking and it all just escalated.

Her husband, Peter, rang me to arrange a visit. I told him I couldn't. I made the excuse that I wanted to remember her how she was. I just didn't want to be in that environment because of my mental state (and I didn't have anything I could say to her that would make things better).

So, I just said 'I want to remember her how she was, Peter.' Which was chicken shit.

I like to think that, if she'd have asked for me, Peter would have told me, and I would have gone. I like to think so, anyway.

When she went, that was it for my health anxiety. It was incredible how quick it took hold. Every spot I would be fretting, thinking 'that's cancer'.

It got so I couldn't shower in the daytime, or with the light on, so I wouldn't see any spots on my body that would panic me. You try having a shower in the pitch dark. It's not easy or pleasant.

I'd get a spot and it could be anything, an in-growing hair or just a spot, it wouldn't look like a developing cancer, but I would still fret about it. With that extra vigilance you'll see spots you've never seen before that have always been there.

I remember the first time I saw the liver spots on my hand. Suddenly, they were there, and I was terrified.

I even stood over a mirror checking my anus to see if anything was there. Of course, when you look at your anus for the first time, (should you want to, of course) there's all sorts there, crinkling, all sorts. It isn't pretty. I'd do it, go away, and thirty seconds later and I'd be back and checking it again.

It was constant. I went through eighteen months of CBT, but it didn't work. I had another twenty-six weeks of it recently – again, a minute improvement.

I've seen cancerous spots and they don't look good, or anything like a spot I had. I can be 99% convinced that a spot isn't anything. But that won't stop me fretting about it and I need reassurance, or someone else to check it for me.

I remember going to my GP, who's also a surgeon, certificates all over his walls, rightly proud of all he's achieved.

"I work a hundred hours a week Stephen…" he'd always say to me.

This time I came in and he greeted me;
"Ah, Stephen! How are you my friend?"
"I'm alright."
"Are you alright Stephen?" he said, "Are you alright? What can we do for you then?"
"Can you check inside my mouth?" I can hear myself saying it now. It still sounds ridiculous.
"You want me to look inside your mouth?" he said, sceptical but amused, "What for?"

"Cancer."

He turned around and started typing on his computer 'He wants me to check inside his mouth!' before turning back to me.

"How many times have you been here in the last six months? Do you know?" he asked, "Sixty-eight. Sixty-eight times in the last six months. How many red flags can you seen on my screen? Do you know what a red flag is?"

"I can guess…"

"None." He said, "Come to my surgery Tuesday morning. Sit in my waiting room for four hours. See all the people that are dying. You're not dying."

"What about this discolouration in my eyes?"

"Look in my eyes Stephen, what do you see?" of course his eyes were all red and bloodshot, because of age, "You're not twenty-five anymore. What do you think it is? Cancer?"

"Yeah."

"One in three of us will get cancer. One in three. You have to accept that."

"I don't want to get it," I pleaded, "I don't want to die, I want to live forever."

"You're not going to live forever."

"Alright, I want to live to 97 then,"

"You might not," Dr Kumar shrugged, "You might die today."

"Don't tell me that!"

"If you want to live so much, why do you want to live miserable?" I've had that said to me by a few consultants over the years. "You've spent the last eight years panicking. What's happened in the last eight years? Nothing. What a waste. What a waste of a life."

But it doesn't matter how many times they tell you.

My therapy now is non-avoidance, dealing with the fear and trying not to respond or do anything about it. And it's not easy.

I've suffered with this my entire life and it's tiring. You're constantly fatigued. And because you're constantly fatigued, your body rebels. And because your body rebels and you constantly body scan, you're constantly feeling something that's not comfortable. Because it's not comfortable you're then anxious and that exacerbates the feeling of uncomfortableness and anxiety.

From the minute I wake up to the minute I go to bed, at least once a minute I body scan or think about something to do with my health. Every single day.

My head feels full and fuzzy because there's no room in it for anything else. It only takes something stressful and I'm gone.

I've lived with that my whole life and it's tiring. I have probably seen about five different psychiatrists and been diagnosed at various times with clinical depression, bipolar disorder, manic depression, general anxiety disorder, hypochondria and psychoses. I've been prescribed Fluoxetine, Seroxat, Citalopram, Sertraline, Venlafaxine, Amitriptyline, Lorazepam, Propranolol and now, Mirtazapine. It doesn't work miracles for my mood, but it keeps me on an even keel, for which I'm thankful.

With my acting, being on stage was an extension of needing to be loved, wanting to be the centre of attention, wanting to be liked. But being in a band was something else. The band came together while I was deep in the throes of my health anxiety and I needed it in my life. Something to distract me.

It came together through some strange coincidences, as some things do.

A few years ago, I was a manager at this retail store and the managers had to stand up and give a talk about something they did. I'd just started learning the drums because someone I knew had been doing it and I thought I'd give it a bash.

So, I got up and said I played drums, although I'd only had one lesson at the time.

Afterwards this guy came up to me and said;

"I'm in a band. We need a drummer."

I was gutted.

"I can't play," I had to admit; "I've only just started."

'Fucking hell,' I thought, 'I could've been in a band.'

And that was the end of that. Or so I thought,

After I left that job, I got a call from that same guy.

"Are you still playing drums?" he said, "Do you still write songs? Do you want to write some original stuff with me and form a band?"

Of course, the answer was yes to everything.

And that was how Shock of the Fall started.

That guy is Neil, our lead guitarist and the two of us often say, 'Remember that time when you couldn't play? And look at us now!'

Me and Neil are the original members and Karl, who I consider one of my few close friends, is the other member who's been in the band since early doors.

I got Facebooked by a guy who used to occasionally bully me on the Brum (HMS Birmingham). We both did boxing; he was a middleweight and I was a light welterweight, but we trained well together. It's funny, maybe it was just my perspective or maybe he changed, but as soon we Facebooked, he was glad to hear from me, and started reminiscing about the old days. Maybe he never really bullied me? Maybe he just wasn't what I wanted him to be?

He told me he remembered how I used to be able to be able to sit down, bend over and put my head on my knees. Those days are gone. I told him these days I can barely put my hand on my knees!

I imagine a normal person would look back on that with fondness, but I look back with sadness. I always tell myself I never look back but when I do look back it's with a sense of melancholy.

Recently I got I touch with a girl I went out with when I was 14. She sent me a picture of my name carved on a brick outside her house (which is still there to this day).

"Do you remember that?" she asked, "You were my first love," She said. It made me feel sad. I never knew that.

I told her how looking back made me feel sad.

"Oh, I don't," she said, "I feel glad to have seen you again. You should remember it with fondness."

And I know I should. But I don't.

The Dark Side

There were certain times in my life, when things got too much, I would self-harm or go on drinking binges which would put me in the sickbay. In hindsight I was never far from the edge of the abyss but it's quite hard to see it sometimes…..

I wrote a poem when I was in MCTC, on the way out of the Navy. It summed up a lot of what I was going through at the time, even though I probably didn't even fully realise it. Here is part of it…

Endless roads I have walked,
Out of touch with reality,

To endless people I have talked,
But never heard anyone else but me,

In Endless beds I have slept,
Shared my body but not my soul,

Endless promises I never kept,
And I wonder why I wander alone.

I read it now and I think 'that was me then'. When I wrote that poem it was easy, it just came out. For someone who was 20 to write that, I thought it was quite deep. And showed I knew something about myself.
Even then, despite everything, I felt that I was an emotional vacuum in some respects.

It was like a paradox. I was liked but I didn't like myself. I was liked, I was successful at what I wanted to do, but I thought to myself; "You're not, are you?"

The dark side was always there, even when I didn't notice it, all through the good times. Some parts from this period I still have no memory of.

When I was first thinking of writing this book, around ten years ago, I wrote off for and got my naval records, which were just in date at the time. Some of the things I read in there were a real shock.

At some point in Portsmouth I got an STD – Gonorrhoea. They sent me to an STD clinic and did a question and answer survey with me, as they try to track down the source or stop the spread, as it impacts on the ship, if it spreads there. Really it's a damage limitation exercise.

They did the umbrella thing with me. I think of it and even now get that sinking feeling in the pit of my stomach. They push it down your urethra, press the button and then it flicks open and they drag out any shit there, while you're stood there holding your bits open. Fucking hell, it's horrible.

When I got my naval records back there was a note in the records about the incident. They always refer to you as 'this young sailor' in the third instance; they never use your name.

In the Naval record they'd asked me questions at the clinic, and it said, 'this young sailor recounted 8 partners over the weekend of xx/xx/xx' and then it said, in capitals, 'AND HE CAN'T EVEN REMEMBER THEIR NAMES'.

I would have been in my early forties when I first read this. It was like reading about another person. I was just thinking 'fucking hell! That is really awful'. It was painful to read but I knew that that was what I was like back then.

I couldn't remember anybody. I knew the pubs I'd been in, because they were my locals, but I couldn't remember any of the people I'd been with.

That last sentence has stuck with me since then. I thought 'what must people have thought of me?' Not the women I was with, because, as far as I'm aware, everyone I was with had a decent time. But the people on the periphery who must have looked at me and thought, 'this isn't a good guy, this guy'.

This was a bit of a shock to me, but nothing like the shock of reading the notes of me going to a psychiatrist, which said that I'd been putting needles into my abdomen. I had no recollection of doing that. None whatsoever.

I do remember one visit to a psychiatrist, and it relates to something that happened during my basic training.

At that time, they were making a training video, to go out worldwide, and I was due to sit at the front. I was thinking 'Fucking hell, brilliant! I'll be in a video!'

Somebody was looking at me, at my name badge, and called me over.

The main guy that was the actor for the video, was a sailor called Joe Utting, which is quite a rare name – it's originally Bavarian, (Utting, that is – not Joe!) I believe.

But because Joe was in the video, I was told I couldn't be, so they sent me to the back. It was a frustrating, ridiculous coincidence, but not as bad as what came later.

Years later, after the needles in the abdomen and the cry for help, I was sent to see a psychiatrist.

"Right, come in Joe…" He said as I entered the room.

"My name's not Joe."

"Is your name Utting?"

"Yeah."

"Joe Utting?"

I couldn't believe it. They hadn't even got my records right. It wasn't even me. They'd call me in there to get help and that wasn't even me. I had thirty stitches in my wrist. I was a mess.

And the psychiatrist just went;

"Ah, do you know what," he looked down at the wrong paperwork with disgust, "Shall we just forget it?"

I was just thinking, 'You can't even get my name right! How are you going to help me?' And of course, he didn't. He just binned it off.

Although I was still enjoying my hedonistic life there were moments that made me wonder what I was doing.

There was one time in the Vic Bars in Weymouth where I was downstairs with a woman I'd just met, a onetime thing, in one of the American style booths. While we were talking she just suddenly said;

"Ooh, my nipples are really hard..."

Even though I'd just picked her up, I didn't expect it to go so quickly from chatting up to sex, I was just thinking 'Wow...!'

So, she asked me to take her outside and fuck her, or words to that effect.

"Yeah, alright," I said, knowing the beach was over the road.

"In the bus shelter." She said.

It was a glass fronted bus shelter, right on the road. There were people wondering round with bags of chips.

"That's where I want you to do it," she said, "That's where I want to do it. In the bus shelter in the middle of the road."

So that's where I did it.

"Talk dirty to me," she said as we got started, "Louder!"

I could hear people thinking, 'Fucking hell! Look at that! What's going on there?!'

That also makes me think of Tina, the student in Weymouth, who was a scratcher and biter. When I was going out with her I remember lying on the seafront, on the pavement just in front of the beach.

This woman and man walked past, and I heard her whisper; 'John! John! Look at that man's back!'

And at the time I thought 'Yeah.' Like it was a badge of honour. But it must have looked a right mess. I have conflicting thoughts, but I can't help but wonder, if that were my lad, how I'd feel about that badge of honour.

There was another girl in Weymouth, a big Amazonian woman, statuesque. I took her to bed and spent an hour banging her, everything I could think of, I was sweating buckets. Throughout, I was thinking, 'fucking hell, Steve. You're doing a right good job here.'

I'll always remember, at the end she said, dissatisfied;

"Do you know, I always like my men to give that little bit more, to make the earth move."

And I just thought 'Fucking hell!' I couldn't get my breath, 'Really?'

As it turned out, when I left her, she locked herself in the toilet with bottles of brandy threatening to take an overdose.

And I was thinking, "Hang on a minute, I'm not giving you what you want. Except I clearly am, or you wouldn't be threatening to do that."

That was probably one of the few times there was an after effect to the relationship ending. In a way that made me quite hard, when that wasn't what I was normally like, thinking 'You've criticised me on the one hand and then when I try to move on, you've done this…?'

But 99% of the time when I ended a relationship with someone it was good. I could go into that bar night after night after night and not get any grief from anybody, whether I've slept with them the night before or not. I guess we all wanted the same thing.

I remember at one point in Portsmouth consciously thinking that it was too easy for me, pulling and getting women, and saying to myself that I needed a challenge. It seems a bit narcissistic looking back, a really low thing to do. But there it is.

I don't know why, and I don't know how I thought of it, but I decided to give myself a real challenge. I decided to pull a girl while being mute. I said to myself 'I'm going to pull by being mute. I'm going to pull without saying anything'.

I didn't go in any of my local pubs, the ones I normally went in, I went in this different pub, afternoon, sunny day, with a notepad and a pencil.

I went in, looked round and saw a couple of young girls sat at a table and then went up to the bar.

"What can I get you?" the barman asked.

And so, I wrote in the notepad.

Pint of bitter please

"Oh man," he said, sympathetic, "You can't speak, you can't- ?"

I shook my head sadly.

By this time, I could see these girls looking. One of them came up.

"Are you alright? Are you ok?" she said.
Yeah I wrote on my notepad.
"What's up?" she asked.
Accident at work I wrote.
She went back to her friends and talked with her for a bit and then went off. One of her friends came over to me and said.
"She's gone for a bit of a weep. She's really upset. Do you want to come and sit with us?"
Yeah, ok.

So, I went and sat down with them. Now you wouldn't realise how hard not speaking is. And I played that role for two hours. Then one of the girls said;
"There's a fair on the seafront, would you like to go to the fair?"
Yeah, I would. Ring me.
"How will you answer the phone?"
And suddenly I was thinking, 'Good point, how will I answer the phone?'
I'll get my friend to answer it.
We made the arrangements and I went to the fair a few days after. Again, you try going on a fairground ride without making a noise. It's hard!
I didn't have sex with them; I just had a really good time. And that was that. At the end of it, I made whatever excuse it was and then didn't see them again.

Weeks later I was in the Mighty Fine, sat where I was normally sat, disco booths just to one side, surrounded by women, people I've had sex with, people I've had relationships with, having a great time. Then these two girls walk in.
It was the first time I'd ever seen them in the Mighty Fine. They came over and obviously heard me speaking.
I don't remember their exact words, but it was along the lines of 'You bastard!'
I couldn't think of anything to say. There was nothing to say. I was genuinely speechless this time.
All I could say was that I was sorry and that I never meant to hurt anyone. I couldn't tell them it was a challenge. I didn't do it with any

malice aforethought; I just did it to see if I could do it. But that was one of those times I felt really small and just thought 'this is not good is it?'

There was a girl who used to drink in the Mighty Fine, who I really fancied, called Fran. One Sunday afternoon she said, 'do you want to come back to mine for a drink?' Obviously I thought; 'Yes! I'm in!'
We went back to her flat in Nightingale Road, where I'd already been in five or six of those flats with different women. I'd had a drink and started talking and she suddenly said.
"I ain't sleeping with you."
I was brought up short, but I said;
"Yeah, yeah, alright…"
"You're here for a drink and a chat," she said, "I ain't sleeping with you, because you're a slag."
I don't know what I said to that. I know I didn't stay long afterwards though but, with hindsight, and as the years goes on, the impact of it was powerful.
"You sleep with everyone," she said, as if it was a bad thing. Up until then, I'd thought it was the thing to do, "You ain't sleeping with me."
As I say, I don't think I stayed long after that. But it was an eye opener, that not everybody thought the same.
Throughout my life I've always wrestled with my morality. Some people have told me that I was only doing what young guys do but I struggled to see it that way.
I got to about 20 and thought 'I need to stop this. I need to wake up and feel different.' Maybe I'd had an overload, but when I left the Navy all I wanted was to get married and settle down.
It took a lot of therapy and feeling guilty about what I'd done until, years later, I spoke to a woman counsellor who asked me;
"Did you enjoy it?"
"Yeah."
"Did they enjoy it?"
"I think so."
"Did you consciously set out to hurt anybody?"
"No…"

"And did everybody have a good time?"
"Yeah…."
"So, what have you done wrong?"
I didn't have an answer to that.

I was constantly looking for acceptance and constantly beating myself down. Even now I do the same, constantly running down what I do.

I don't have many friends, even now; I'm quite closed and insular in general. I guess it is an esteem issue at times.

Back in the Navy, like I've said, I usually went out alone. There was one moment where I got a glimpse of what it would be like to have friends, or comrades. I was out, in Portsmouth I think, and I was dancing with a local girl. A local guy came up to me and started play dancing with me, holding me, with a view to kneeing me in the nuts.

I could tell something was coming, with my martial arts training, so I had my side on and my knee up. If he'd have got me in the nuts it would have really hurt though.

At that point, one of my ship mates, Jock, or Axe-in-the-Head, came over. I've mentioned already that he was a nutter, and a big tall guy, but he was a good guy to have on your side.

Jock went over to the local and told him he'd better fuck off or he'd do him. I looked over to him;

"Thanks Jock!"

"No trouble!"

It was like a window into what it must feel like to have friends looking out for you.

But at the time I liked solitude most of all. That was probably why I always did Christmas duties. I probably went home for Christmas once in the four and a half/five years I was in and instead I'd volunteer for Christmas duties. I used to like being on my own on the ship with a skeleton crew, doing a bit of maintenance and the like.

I remember one Christmas, over two weeks, watching probably every Elvis film. They had an Elvis film on every morning, and I remember it being real escapism.

The Christmas duties on the camps one year, were just me patrolling around the camp perimeter at night, just thinking to myself how cool it was, how peaceful and full of solitude.

I used to quite like my own company, which is odd because I was in a team environment, but I seemed to get on better with myself. And I seemed to get on better with civvies than I did with Navy guys. I don't know why.

But that was who I was then. The person I wrote about in my poem Endless.

.... And now

So, after nearly sixty years, I have almost learned to live with just being me. And although I may not have dealt all the cards I was given, I certainly played them and attach no blame to anyone but me for the consequences.

I still suffer with mental health issues – mainly health anxiety and depression but I have learned to live with them – along with the medication and their side effects.

I have a small group of people I am glad to call friends, and my social circle is a lot bigger than it used to be.

Shock Of The Fall is still going strong and it forms a massive part of my life and well-being. We have gigged at the O2 Academy – twice – and it's as near to 'living the dream' as I'm going to get, I guess. Again, I'm grateful for it. I also find song writing – especially writing lyrics, cathartic and 'good to get out'.

I have been involved in music promotion in some small part and really enjoy meeting talented people who emote through their music. I have also been involved in helping to organise my local music festival for the past few years and thanks to Steve P for asking me in the first place. There is nothing like the buzz of live music to make you feel better about the world.

As part of my sixtieth birthday, my daughter took me to Liverpool for the night and we ended up in the world-famous Cavern Club, where I managed to play with the house band for a number – we did I Can't Explain by The Who. It was a packed house and the crowd sang happy birthday to me after our song. Winner, winner!

I have a better relationship with my mum than I ever did – we don't spend much time together but when we do, its pleasant. I think time, age and life experience all play a part in that. I have bridges that are forever burned but hey-ho, I imagine lots of people do. I try not to dwell on what ifs too much.

I am still living on my own – ten years and counting and if I think about it too much, I get lonely at times. But as with most things, if I really wanted to change it, I could. Who knows?

Materially, I have everything I could want. But I still get maudlin occasionally, when I watch a tearjerker or hear a heartfelt song. Us humans being blessed with self-awareness isn't always a blessing.

But, all in all, I am happy with my lot and try not to be too introspective. Sometimes it's good to just *do* and not sweat the small stuff.

I remember well the roads I walked,

I see them much more clearly now.

Maybe I'll listen when people talk,

And forget endless times I never knew how.